RACE,
PROPAGANDA
AND
SOUTH AFRICA

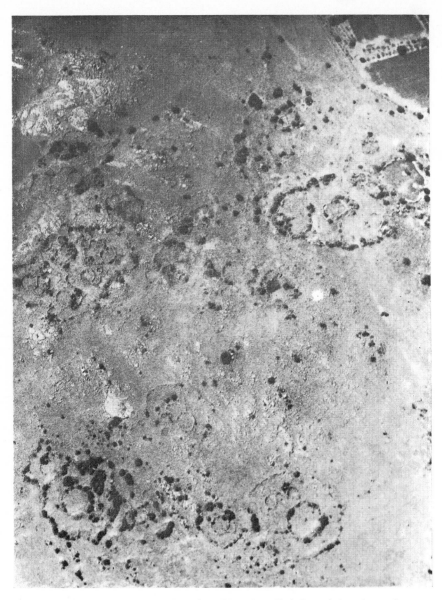

Eighty-six per cent of South Africa is officially claimed to be historically "white"— that is, never settled by blacks (Bantu). Yet much of this "white" land, including this section abutting a white farm near Johannesburg, bears large stone kraals whose archaeological dating proves centuries of pre-white settlement by blacks (see Chapter Three). (*Aerial photograph, scale* 1 *in.* = 150 *ft. approx.*)

RACE,
PROPAGANDA
AND
SOUTH AFRICA

by

JOHN C. LAURENCE

LONDON
VICTOR GOLLANCZ LTD
1979

© John C. Laurence 1979
ISBN 0 575 02691 X

MADE AND PRINTED IN GREAT BRITAIN BY
THE GARDEN CITY PRESS LIMITED
LETCHWORTH, HERTFORDSHIRE SG6 1JS

"Truth is what people believe. It has very little to do with fact."—*United States Republican Party Workshop Training Manual for Politicians' Press Secretaries, quoted in the London* Sunday Times, *30 April 1978.*

"People act according to what they think the facts are. But they live or die in accordance with what the facts really are."—*Anon.*

To : the thousand or so South Africans of all races who are currently banned and silenced without trial, so that nothing they say or write may be quoted in their own country; nor may they travel abroad to state their case to the Free World.

AUTHOR'S NOTE

In view of official action taken against journalists at times in southern Africa, it should be mentioned that no journalist of the same or similar name who is or has at any time been working there is in any way connected with the author.

CONTENTS

CONTENTS

INTRODUCTION

THE SECOND HALF of the twentieth century has, above all else, been the age of mass communication. As television has rapidly dominated the homes and leisure time of the Western world, and the Third World has become increasingly literate, the power of the mass media (newspapers, magazines, television and radio) and of those who control it—whether politicians or private citizens—has become unsuspectedly vast. So much so that the old saying, "The pen is mightier than the sword", is now rephrased by some professional newsmen as "the pen decides who will use the sword, against whom, and when".

Perhaps such newsmen are not as cynical as they seem, for the post-war years have seen the rise not only of the all-pervading power of the mass media—with their instant news reports and often equally instant "informed comment"—but also of the power of the lobbyist and the propagandist, both economic and political. The techniques of multi-million-dollar public-relations and advertising consultants are today not only being used to monitor and control public taste in breakfast cereals. They are being used increasingly for political, economic and even racial indoctrination, often camouflaged as "objective information".

In the still relatively free societies of the West, this fact is now generally recognized. But the question immediately arises: if the great issues of the day have in fact become the football of squads of professional persuaders, whom does one believe? Where does the truth exist, and how does one find it?

The question is no mere rhetoric, for in November 1978 the President of the United States had to ask it of his own intelligence service, the most widespread and heavily financed in the world. Although American private citizens and government officials alike had for years had free access to Iran, to such a degree that the country was considered "safe" enough to purchase billions of dollars' worth of US arms and thus alter the balance of power in the front line against Russia, President Carter was suddenly forced to send "an angry hand-written note to the CIA expressing his dissatisfaction with the failure of US intelligence to forecast the turmoil in Iran"—just three months after the CIA had assured him that "Iran is not in a revolutionary or pre-revolutionary situation".

The nation which more than any other is supposed to understand the modern arts both of communication and anti-communication had suffered a total information breakdown. And this despite the fact that a similar, earlier failure had helped bring about the Vietnam disaster, and that America's current policies in Africa were showing ample signs of being based on inaccurate information and faulty interpretations.

In that same month of November 1978, by an odd coincidence, events in South Africa were giving a very clear hint as to why America's—and other Western countries'—policies towards the white minority states of southern Africa were proving to be so embarrassingly ill-informed and inept, and why the British people had been so easily deceived over a period of more than ten years about the rather obvious fact that despite international sanctions, rebel Rhodesia had been getting nearly all the oil and petrol it needed.

In South Africa, due to the courage of one judge and a handful of newspapermen, it was revealed that not only was an important department of the government corrupt, but that the form that corruption had taken was illegally to use state funds to finance more than one hundred "front" organizations for the pro-apartheid government propaganda machine both inside and outside South Africa; and that the main thrust of this exercise had been aimed—and indeed is still aimed—at controlling allegedly impartial news sources in South Africa, Britain and America and turning them into unsuspecting broadcasters of South African racial, political and economic propaganda, giving the views solely of the small white minority.

That this propaganda was—and is—no mere mild persuasion based on legitimate interpretations of the facts is shown in considerable detail throughout this book. South African propaganda—spread by government sources and hundreds of private organizations alike—is based on major distortions of the facts of economics, employment, racial discrimination, politics and even history. These distortions have been accepted again and again by the policy-makers of the white West as the insecure foundations on which to base almost all their policies towards South

Africa and even Rhodesia. And the distortions are still being disseminated by South Africa and still being accepted by the West as "the facts", as a perusal of the central chapters of this book should make sufficiently clear.

Yet there is another aspect which has barely been touched on before in any of the hundreds of books and thousands of articles and broadcasts about South Africa over recent years. This is that the West is preconditioned, so to speak, to accept South African racial propaganda simply because both the West and the ruling, all-powerful minority in South Africa are in effect white.

This is a subject with so many complexities and nuances that this author admits that only after more than ten years of examining South African racial propaganda and its repetition in the West's mass media and parliaments, a study conducted both in South Africa and Britain, did the picture finally become clear enough to write about. The mechanism of bias—almost always unconscious bias—which is at work here is dealt with in some detail in Chapter One, but a foretaste of what is involved can do no harm here.

Briefly, much of the failure of the white West's mass media— and politicians—to see through the fog of tacitly anti-black South African racial propaganda seems to boil down to this: while many a Protestant (for instance) has come to fully understand the Catholic point of view by becoming a Catholic; and while many a Communist has easily come to understand capitalism by becoming a capitalist; no white man has ever become a black man. So those influential white people in the West who *think* they understand black Africa may in truth be almost totally miscomprehending it. And the miscomprehension is made greater still by white-made communication barriers such as South African apartheid.

There are thus two massive barriers to the white West's understanding of what is really happening in southern Africa. The first is the distortions of South African racial propaganda— the skilled barrage of misinformation doubtless still being surreptitiously injected in even greater quantities into Western society by South Africa's now partly-revealed Trojan Horses of "bought" newspapers, magazines and even journalists. The second is the information barrier erected by the white minorities between the white West and the black majorities in southern Africa—the white hand across the black mouths. And there is also a third barrier in the form of the comprehension gap between black and white.

This last barrier conceals more than just information. It conceals black feelings, attitudes, plans—and the degree to which the large black majorities in southern Africa are reaching breaking-point under the white yoke, whether this yoke is direct, or applied by remote control. In view of the more than five billion pounds of British money alone in southern Africa, the existence of these feelings, attitudes and crunch-points is important (quite apart from the moral aspect). Yet it has been largely ignored by the West, although its reality and nature can be glimpsed easily enough by asking one short question : Would the white West still be so anxious to co-exist with South Africa if that country were a place where 4.3 million *blacks* oppressed 23 million *whites*—and shot unarmed white schoolchildren in the back when they protested against their unequal education?

The question is a legitimate one. For more than a decade of daily study of comment about southern Africa in most of Britain's major newspapers and television programmes has revealed, in 1978, a growing emotional commitment to the white cause in southern Africa, coupled with a distinct disinclination to give any but the whites' side of the question, or even to test some of the white minorities' claims against the rules of simple arithmetic.

Of Rhodesia, for instance, both the British and American news media have happily repeated Mr Ian Smith's claims that his internal agreement and election were based on "one man, one vote"—while the actual text of the agreement of 3 March 1978 proves that 28 per cent of parliamentary seats for Rhodesia's four per cent white minority is really "one black man, one vote; one white man, nine votes".

Mr Smith's three-week visit to America in October 1978 neatly coincided with another example of Rhodesian misinformation instantly echoed by the West's mass media. During his visit it was announced that the "Internal Government" was to renounce all forms of racial discrimination. No one seems to have mentioned that that left Rhodesia racially shared out on the basis of roughly twenty times more land for a white than for a black, under the unrevoked 1930 Land Apportionment Act.

South Africa's unilateral election in Namibia in December

of the same year produced a similarly one-sided spate of reporting. Nearly all reports in Britain claimed there had been no intimidation of the mostly black voters, and that the 81 per cent poll showed that Namibians rejected SWAPO. Few news media carried the facts that the UN Special Representative had some weeks earlier been advised by church leaders in Namibia that registration of black voters had been carried out under duress, and that "registration receipts were essential to get jobs and medical treatment". Or that the inevitably high poll was not a secret one, white officials observing how each black Namibian voted, while the main white party's officials were the only ones allowed—by the white minority administration—to carry guns at the polling booths.

Perhaps the white West's growing emotional bias towards whites in southern Africa is the more worrying because several experienced observers have suggested that in some areas it is already similar to the total overthrow of reason observed in, for instance, the British press during the first few months of both world wars. The evidence of massive public reaction in the white West to the murder of groups of whites in Rhodesia by blacks, but the almost complete indifference to the murder of much larger number of blacks by whites, can be found in almost any newspaper. Certainly, in many cases the white deaths were closer to atrocities, but the phenomenon was also observed where the deaths of blacks were the less excusable.

There is, too, a much-closer-to-home aspect of the anti-black attitudes thus encouraged by the West's mass media and politicians alike: the effect on Britain's and America's black minorities of such selective reporting and comment. However, this aspect is not dealt with at any great length in this book, as the author feels that others are more qualified to comment on it.

Even so, much ground is covered in the pages that follow, and some might disagree with the sequence of subjects chosen. There is a quite logical progression, however, as follows: It is felt to be important to establish the groundswell of unsuspected racial bias in the West before leading in to the way South African propaganda and lobbying operations have made use of this, and have permeated even the parliaments of the West with their usually unsuspected tentacles. Following this is a carefully documented series of chapters exposing the main propaganda themes of white South Africa, and comparing the claims made with the essential facts. Throughout, some attempt is made to illustrate the black South African viewpoints which the propaganda conceals, and this subject is more fully developed in the final chapter.

But the core of the book is its central chapters, nevertheless, for these try to set out in some detail the answers to three important questions: If South Africa's extraordinary plans for secretly gaining editorial control of key sections of the West's major news sources had been fully successful, exactly what would such subverted members of the free world's mass media have been telling their readers and viewers about South Africa? How far does such propaganda diverge from the truth, and with what purpose? And—since this propaganda has already been (and is still being) more overtly spread throughout the world by a variety of South African agencies over the past fifteen years or more—what has been the effect of such misinformation on public opinion, foreign policy and even black/white race relations in the nations of the West?

PART ONE

THE MECHANICS OF MISINFORMATION

CHAPTER ONE

Racial Bias and the Mass Media

NEWSPAPER AND TELEVISION people are, not surprisingly, very sensitive to allegations of bias in their news reports, articles and programmes, and this is especially true where racial bias is concerned. Yet it would be foolish to pretend that such bias is always absent. In the last two or three years alone, for instance, articles have appeared in respectable British newspapers which twist the facts of science so as to suggest that black and white human beings belong to different species, as a preface to anti-black remarks masquerading as legitimate comment.

This chapter is mainly concerned with less obvious racial bias in the media, and indeed in the English language itself. Bias that is unsuspected even by the most respected newspaper and television newsmen and commentators who possess it and spread it, simply because it is an unconscious function of their heritage, culture, environment—and white race. And it is further unsuspected because not only those in the mass media, but the politicians and general public, suffer from it as well.

Such bias is a reality, although the degree to which it exists is probably a matter of argument. Many examples of it are offered in the pages which follow, because it appears to be a subject which has been largely ignored whenever racial matters and racial confrontations are discussed. Yet because it affects both the reactions to, and reporting of, such racial affairs, it needs to be brought into the open. For it may well be a precondition of racism itself, and it certainly affects one's ability to understand the nature and dangers of racial propaganda.

To give a recent British example : most people should find the following comments, made by an angry British MP in parliament, sufficiently familiar to even name the speaker and the race of the people to whom he referred. He spoke of British "schools crowded with foreign children ... the very posters and advertisements on the wall in a foreign tongue . . . the rates overburdened with the education of thousands of children of foreign parents".[1] And more in similar vein.

Few people now alive should really recognize that statement, for it was made in Britain's parliament in 1902 by a Conservative MP in the course of complaining about the large numbers of *Jewish* immigrants being allowed into Britain to settle. Yet in 1978 a British Conservative MP of *Jewish* parentage was telling Jewish voters in Britain that they should have "good reason" for supporting a further cut-back in immigration proposed by his party. But this time, the "foreign children" and "foreign parents" were mostly not "foreign" at all, but members of the British Commonwealth. Their skins, however, were brown and black. So the offspring of one non-British immigrant group have been telling other immigrants that they are not welcome—and apparently seeing nothing odd in their attitude to immigrants of a different race from their own.

A discussion on coloured immigration into Britain is not a proper part of this book, all the same, because it is less concerned with criticizing public attitudes on race than with trying to distinguish between fact and prejudice on that subject—between informed comment and the unintelligent repetition of other people's prejudices. And this subject, too, lends itself to a recent, well-known example of the way in which people who sincerely consider themselves not to be racially prejudiced can nevertheless publicly exhibit racial double standards. In Britain, early 1978 was a time of two important national debates, both primarily concerned with race. One was about "what to do" with Britain's four per cent of coloured people, the other, whether to accept certain much-publicized settlement terms negotiated within Rhodesia by its four per cent of white people. Not only is the size of the racial minority identical in both cases, but the two minorities are mostly immigrants—that is, most coloured Britons were born outside Britain, and most white Rhodesians were born outside Rhodesia. And almost everybody involved was a member of the British Commonwealth in one way or another, while each minority was making a worthwhile contribution to its host country.

Rarely have two demographic situations been so closely matched, and probably never have they both come to public attention at exactly the same time—offering an opportunity under almost "laboratory" conditions to test for racial double standards. For if racial double standards are truly absent, one should find at least some points of basic similarity in the solutions being put forward to the "problem" of the two racial minorities— coloured in Britain, white in Rhodesia—based on their common humanity.

However, what public-opinion polls and attitude surveys in Britain made clear was this. That on Rhodesia, majority opinion was that the internal agreement should be supported by Britain : that it was right and proper that the four per cent white settler minority should for at least ten years be given at least twenty per cent of seats in parliament; that the whites, but not the blacks, should be asked in a referendum if they approved of these terms; and that one of those terms should be (as made clear in Section A, Clause 2 of the agreement) that Rhodesia's current racial land-shares which gave twenty times more land per head to a white man than to a black man, should continue, and that if blacks wanted more land they would have to pay whites "promptly" for it.

On Britain, British majority opinion was exactly the opposite : the four per cent coloured settler minority did represent some kind of "threat" which might "swamp" white Britons, and so coloured immigration should be severely curtailed as soon as possible, while no special privileges should be allowed this minority.

Such opinions—often echoed even in the more liberal news-papers—speak for themselves. Certainly, it is possible to think up some theory to "explain" this vast difference in attitudes to different races, and so to pretend that they somehow offer no evidence at all of racial prejudice. But there is a simple tech-nique known as Substitution which can be used to show the real size of the gap between such racial attitudes. In this case, one simply substitutes the attitudes towards blacks for those towards whites and vice versa. If racial prejudice is truly absent, it should make little difference. In fact, this is the result :

After such a substitution, one would find the British Con-servative Party, for instance, agreeing to Britain's four per cent coloured minority being given twenty per cent of seats in Britain's parliament for at least ten years; to all coloured pro-perty, even if acquired illegally, being entrenched legally in coloured ownership; and a referendum being held on this agreement in which only the coloured minority, and not the white British majority, would be allowed to vote.

But where Rhodesia is concerned, the Conservative Party would agree that the best solution would be to stop white immigration into Rhodesia to avoid the threat of "swamping" the black majority, and that no special terms at all should be offered now or in the future to Rhodesia's white minority.

It may be argued that such a transposition is unfair. But is it? For the reason the British Conversative Party is specifically mentioned here is that its leader, on the very day on which the British immigration debate really started in 1978, said on television that it was "false" to accuse her party of racial prejudice. The above substitution simply tests that statement at face value.

Clearly, considerable racial confusion can exist even on the subject of Rhodesia, which is British. South Africa, however, is a quite foreign country, so it could be worthwhile, before exploring the largely unfamiliar territory of those aspects of South Africa and apartheid which have largely been lost to view, often being replaced by sophisticated propaganda, to first "learn the language". For there are certain forms of argument, certain key words and phrases, certain semantic slants and twists used in referring to race and to southern Africa which apply a racial bias to language itself. There are also some un-suspected forms of censorship—some traditional and some de-liberate—which further reinforce that racial bias so that even an apparently innocent statement can have a hidden racial warp, or wholly conceal the truth.

Yet this racial bias in human communication applies not only to southern Africa, but to British affairs as well, and is one which can be examined and discussed in great detail. But per-haps the simplest and briefest way to introduce it is to re-publish here an article by this writer, entitled "Censorship by Skin Colour", which was originally published early in 1977 by the international magazine *Index on Censorship*. Some minor alterations have been made to this article and it should be noted that the Miss World Contest referred to now restricts South Africa to one entrant only. Apart from that, almost everything it has to say is still topical.

"In the middle of 1976, soon after the lethal anti-apartheid 'children's war' of South Africa's Soweto township began, a world-renowned television station decided it was time to broad-cast some kind of discussion on the riots. So it assembled a small group of experts to discuss the black violence and its Bantu education background. But none of the experts fully knew what they were talking about, because none had ever been taught even a single lesson in a black South African school, none had ever had to carry a South African 'Pass', and none had ever spent even as much as 24 hours in Soweto—much less actually lived there.

"The reason for their ignorance was simple. All of them were white.

"The black South African has a half-bitter, half-humorous way to describe the consultations, the 'dialogues' and the dis-cussions about racial affairs which cover the realities of apartheid like an ever-present fog : 'The white man is having another *indaba* (tribal meeting) with himself about what to do with us blacks'. There is an ironic truth in this saying—some white South Africans have been known to describe white interdepart-mental discussions about the Bantustans as a 'dialogue with the blacks'. And in that attitude, which finds expression not only in South Africa but in much of the white West, lies the cause of a far-reaching form of censorship which is often not understood or even suspected : censorship by skin colour.

"This censorship operates on two levels—that of Black Ex-clusion and that of Black Viewpoint Exclusion, the latter term being used here to describe the increasingly common phenomenon of a black man, who owes his position and his salary to a ruling white minority, expressing views which on examination turn out to be those of his white masters. That such views are rarely if ever those of the bulk of blacks whom the speaker claims to represent was a point publicly put to the test in 1972. White 'experts' and black Rhodesian chiefs alike forecast a strong 'Yes' vote for the Smith/Home independence proposals. But the black Rhodesians themselves, once the gag of racial censorship was re-moved, voted a resounding 'No'.

"Black Exclusion, however, remains the most common way of censoring the real aims and opinions of subject races from the West's press and television. A good example occurred in October 1976—the month of the Transkei Bantustan's alleged indepen-dence and so a time of heavy coverage of the black/white con-frontation in southern Africa, a part of the world where blacks outnumber whites by some five to one, and there are actually more literate blacks than literate whites.

"Of 'serious' British national daily newspapers, the one with the highest circulation by far is the *Daily Telegraph*. A check through that newspaper's October 1976 issues (one issue was missed) was made, with a view to assessing the racial standpoint and sources of editorials, chat-columns and articles, plus that of letters published. Of around a dozen articles and staff comments on southern African racial affairs, none was pro-black, and all but one were emphatically pro-white. Of the letters published, five were pro-black and thirteen pro-white. (The terms 'pro-white' and 'pro-black' are necessarily simplifications : account was taken of racial attitudes generally, perhaps the main one being whether the writer concerned felt that southern African blacks should be ruled by themselves, or by whites.)

"The *Telegraph* itself might dispute the precise figures, but the overall pro-white standpoint is very clear. Even so, the *Daily Telegraph* might well argue that in a Britain where 95 per cent of the population is white, a pro-white viewpoint is not very remarkable. But in fact, that was not the main reason why this small piece of research was done.

"It was done in order to find out whether, in a period of massive public interest in southern Africa, any of the millions of literate blacks or dozens of able black journalists in that part of the world had been invited to speak through the pages of an important British newspaper. And the answer was very clear— all the comment on black southern Africa was written by whites.

"The *Daily Telegraph* has merely been used as an example here—most British media behave in exactly the same way. With rare exceptions, the black man's voice about his own black affairs is simply 'censored' out of British media—and this despite the fact that there are hundreds of articulate black Rhodesians and black South Africans in Britain who know better than most white journalists exactly what is happening in their countries, but whom the media rarely make any attempt to approach.

"It might, of course, be argued that this is not evidence of any anti-black bias—of any definite refusal to let the black man have his say—in British media. But there is a simple test that can be applied to this situation. Where Russian racism against Jews is concerned, do British media show a similar re-

luctance to open their columns, microphones and TV studios to
Jewish people here who have experienced Russian racism at first
hand? Is it not in fact true that in such cases, our mass media
(quite rightly) do make an effort to present the victims' viewpoint from the victims' own mouths? And if so, why the dif-
ferential treatment for blacks when black African victims are the
focus of attention? Why is it in such cases that the most common reaction even by the television programmers is to mount a
discussion in which whites talk to whites about what to do with
the blacks?

"The answer most probably lies in a certain obsolescence of
racial viewpoint which most white Westerners possess, and which
is unfortunately also still possessed by the West's opinion-makers.
To coin a phrase, such people still tend to 'think with their skins'.
White skin—'white' thoughts—'white' viewpoint. To take some
more examples, this time from the broadcasting media:

"In October 1976, BBC Radio broadcast two consecutive interviews from South Africa on topical racial matters there. The
first interview, with a white South African cabinet minister, was
'balanced' by an interview with the white leader of South
Africa's all-white main opposition party, the United Party. The
degree of this 'balance' can be assessed by the fact that before
a recent election, the all-white United Party's slogan had been
'We stand for white control over *all* South Africa'. The black
majority was simply ignored, as were all the views and opinions
of that large majority.

"By and large, television coverage of the guerrilla war in
Rhodesia and the township rebellions in South Africa was by
all-white camera crews and white commentators (equivalent,
perhaps, to all the Northern Ireland violence being covered by
all-Protestant ones?). It is firmly denied by the television
authorities themselves that this 'white-only' viewpoint results in
racial bias. But look at two BBC-1 television broadcasts within
three days of each other in mid-November 1976.

"The first, on the 9 pm News on the thirteenth, referred to
African guerrillas as 'terrorists' throughout, and featured film
of Africans serving with Ian Smith's army. They were 'all
volunteers', insisted the (white) commentator, following that
up with 'Their incentives are those of most Africans—regular
pay, regular food—and somewhere to sleep'. For the full flavour
of that statement, simply substitute 'Jews' for 'Africans'. (Or

change 'Africans' to 'whites'—and put the statement in the mouth of a black TV commentator.)

"Three days later, BBC-1 *Tonight* programme offered a classic example of Black Viewpoint Exclusion—a white-made film from Rhodesia featuring a pro-Smith chief who owed not only his position in the Smith government to the white minority, but his modern car and £20,000 a year salary as well. Certainly, the BBC made this quite plain. But in a situation where the majority voice of the black man in southern Africa is an absolute rarity in our media, why show yet another pro-white film? And again, how much enthusiasm—to use a direct analogy—has the BBC shown for searching out pro-Communist Jews in Russia and giving *them* the freedom of the microphone and camera?

"Yet the BBC cannot ultimately be blamed. Thames Television did, shortly after Soweto erupted, put on a fascinating *This Week* half-hour in which, almost for the first time, the real blacks were simply allowed to talk. The TV critics were enthusiastic—but Mr Vorster was less so. When the *This Week* team applied to cover the Transkei's alleged independence, the South African government refused them entry. Thames Television regrettably did not publicize this fact—and so the British public never knew that the reason they saw no in-depth coverage of the Transkei Bantustan's 'independence' in October 1976 was because the South African government had censored British television screens. Simply because some British TV crews refused to censor the black South African majority.

"Specific case-histories have been dealt with in some detail above because it is only too easy to generalize on an often emotional subject; so these offer actual examples of the innocent acceptance of racial stereotypes by the mass media, in a way which censors an entire majority race in the African subcontinent. And often it is found that such racial stereotypes are kept alive by the very language used by the mass media.

"Thus, 'Rhodesian' means 'white' almost invariably, Rhodesians who are not white being described variously as 'blacks' or 'Africans'. (The lunacy of such definitions can be seen by applying the same rules to Britain—in which case only the black British minority becomes 'Britons', all the indigenous whites being called 'whites' or 'Europeans'.)

"Or try some word association: here is a well-known term—

what is the first picture one gets when one reads it? *South African.* Most people's first impression is of a white male. Quite untypical—less than ten per cent of South Africans are white males. Our colourful language is full of such racial bias. Thus :

" 'Rhodesia and South Africa were built up by white skills.' Then why are white Rhodesians allowed to grow and smoke tobacco—surely a 'Red Indian skill'? When even abstract techniques bear racial labels that are used for racist purposes, it is not surprising that tacit racism is so endemic.

"That our language itself can lead not only to racist practices, but to the 'censorship'—i.e., exclusion—of members of other races from profitable enterprises is well illustrated by the history of the 'Miss World' contests.

"For many years, Miss South Africa was chosen only from the one-in-six white minority in that country, apparently due to the word-association syndrome noted above. Eventually world opinion forced a change and, under the largely untenable excuse that apartheid's laws made a non-racial choice of Miss South Africa impossible, it was agreed that two entrants would be accepted in Britain—a Miss South Africa, and a Miss Africa South. The way these two ladies have always been chosen shows how language itself can have bias.

"Miss South Africa is always chosen from whites, and Miss Africa South from 'non-whites'. Leaving aside the fact that the girl chosen from the majority group gets the name of a non-existent country, the splitting up of the South African population into 'whites' and 'non-whites' is crucial to the purpose of white racism, *because it guarantees that a member of the one-in-six white racial minority will always get a bite at the Miss World cake in London every year*—while the members of the other three racial groups in South Africa have no such guarantee. Each group has only a one-third chance.

"In fact, the simplest way to expose this particular racial injustice is to change white racist terms to black racist terms. That is, to divide South Africans up into blacks and non-blacks instead. Then a black girl would always be assured, in the case of two entrants (black and non-black) of getting to the contest in London—but there would be no such assurance for brown or white girls. Once again, the illogic of racism sets the rules— rules so disruptive of human relationships that it would be no more ludicrous for the Miss World Contest to be open only to two classes of girl—English and non-English.

"Such semantic manipulation admittedly has little to do with censorship as such, but it does help to pre-condition people into mental attitudes more conducive to an unwitting acceptance of such practices as racial censorship. (This may be partly because such terms as 'white' and 'non-white' are hidden synonyms for 'pure' and 'impure'. Example : of the three possible racial coup-lings, white/white, white/non-white, and non-white/non-white, only one produces white children—therefore the inherent concept exists that 'non-white' somehow 'taints' white. Significantly, in South Africa where 'white' and 'non-white' are official terms, the white/non-white coupling is actually a criminal offence.)

"However, a further complication to the racial censorship situation *vis-à-vis* South Africa, for instance, lies in communication barriers between people. There are two such important barriers between, say, British people and black South Africans. The first lies in travel restrictions on a racial basis.

"A white Briton can visit South Africa without a visa. A coloured Briton must have a visa (usually refused). And a white South African finds it easy to visit Britain, while a black South African finds it almost impossible. (The *per capita* discrimination here is probably more than 1,000-to-1 against the black South African; South African tourists in Britain, America, Europe etc. being almost always members of the one-in-six white minority.) There is thus a racial people-to-people censorship at work in all contacts between South Africa and the outside world—the reason why the once vaunted 'bridge-building' dialogues with South Africa turned out to be solely between whites and whites.

"But apartheid itself ensures that this same kind of censor-ship also works within South Africa. Anyone who wants to talk to a Russian in Moscow can take him into a coffee-shop and converse for hours. Any white who wants to talk to a black in Johannesburg usually has to use specially reserved areas in certain hotels (talking to blacks on street corners is inadvisable), and invites comment or even police attention if the conversation goes on too long. At all times and in all circumstances, open communication between whites and blacks in South Africa is overtly or covertly inhibited. And when open communication is inhibited, a form of censorship exists, even though it may

. .

be quite unsuspected. Yet surely the fact that it is unsuspected makes its ultimate effect even greater?

"If 'censorship' is defined as a man-made barrier to the free interchange of knowledge and opinion, then does the tacit censorship applied by racial laws in southern Africa and racial attitudes in the white West actually prevent important information from being published and broadcast here? (We are not talking here of South Africa's shrewd 'censorship at source' techniques, whereby newspapers are apparently uncensored but where the most perceptive and well-informed critics of the government—both in South Africa and overseas—are banned or 'named' and may thence not be quoted by the press or any other media in South Africa : a tactic which is known to induce self-censorship in certain overseas journals which depend on sales in South Africa.)

"The tacit censorship induced by obsession with skin colour does, in fact, exist, and some of it has such important effects that it may even alter history, by hiding the feelings and attitudes of other races until those feelings have escalated into action. The example of the almost total 'wrong guess' of white Western journalists as to the outcome of the 1972 Rhodesian Assessment of Opinion has already been given here. But there is another, more serious example, more recent and quite as embarrassing.

"In 1976, *The Times* of London published an article by a capable, senior man about the racial situation in South Africa. The degree to which the author of the article, like every other white journalist in South Africa, appears to have been the victim of unsuspected 'censorship by skin colour' can be judged simply by quoting parts of his article. It should be mentioned that the article was a fair one, but the significant parts are as follows :

I am now leaving South Africa after a six months' stay. . . . Whatever is stirring in South Africa is taking place more among the whites than the blacks. It is not revolution or violence. . . . The two elements indispensable in any popular uprising are both missing in South Africa. One is a deep fury of resentment, and the other is freedom to strike at the governing system. There is no tension in South Africa today as the Middle East and Asia know it. . . . The humour of the working Africans seems to me as fresh and captivating now

as when I grew up among the Zulus . . . if there is a revolution brewing behind those smiles today it is remarkably well
hidden.

"That was published on 14 June 1976. Two days later,
Soweto exploded.

"Was there really no warning at all that South Africa's long
if uneasy slumber was about to turn into nightmare? There
was indeed. Here is one such warning, given publicly just the
month before :

" 'I have a growing nightmarish fear that unless something
drastic is done very soon then bloodshed and violence are going
to happen in South Africa almost inevitably. A people can take
only so much and no more. A people made desperate by despair,
injustice and oppression will use desperate means.'

"The speaker? The Reverend Desmond Tuto, Anglican Dean
of Johannesburg, who is a *black* South African. He was largely
ignored by the white Western press and television, which
favoured instead the more peaceful stories cabled by white
journalists from South Africa. Yet the Rev. Tuto has lived in
Soweto, while not a single white journalist has ever spent as
much as a night there, because the laws of apartheid forbid it.

"Such is the tacit censorship—and the massive misconceptions and misunderstandings—which mere skin colour can produce when it is allowed to influence the flow of information."

The racial bias within our language is in fact rather more far-
reaching than this article's few examples. The point is important because of the very nature of communication itself,
which can most simply be represented as a source, a reception
point, and a medium of communication between the two, such
as pictures, numbers or human language. If the very structure
of this medium of communication is itself biased, then quite
straightforward messages flowing from source to reception point
will frequently be affected by this bias, and themselves become
biased.

Thus, it seems to have escaped the notice of many of the
professional communicators such as journalists and television
commentators that when a white Russian demonstrates against
his government, they call him a "dissident"—but that when a
black South African similarly demonstrates against his govern-

ment, he is called a "militant" or a "radical", or even an "agitator". Which is a language bias.

When South African troops who are illegally in the UN mandated territory of Namibia clashed with armed black Namibians who objected to this foreign control of their country, the blacks were called "guerrillas" or "terrorists". But when white Frenchmen did almost exactly the same thing against the German forces in occupied France during World War II, we called them "resistance heroes".

The London *Times* in 1977 actually described a white woman immigrant in Rhodesia as a "typical Rhodesian", then sharply defended this usage even when it was pointed out that—by strictly accurate analogy—a Pakistani immigrant in Britain is not what one usually means when one speaks of a "typical Briton". *The Times* is not alone in its odd definitions. Many British newspapers use the words "people" and "South Africans" as if they refer only to the white minority in South Africa. Thus, a well-known British journalist on the day of the 1977 "whites only" South African election described apartheid as "a solution which the vast majority of South Africans believe, rightly or wrongly, is the only way of achieving peace and justice within their borders".[2] Yet the true majority of South Africans—the blacks—believe no such thing.

One finds, then, that there is a steady anti-black drift within our very language. And because this augments the untruths, half-truths and evasions of pro-white propaganda—whether from South Africa or from right-wing extremist sources within Britain itself—it makes the work of all such white racial propagandists that much easier and more effective.

Yet it must be admitted that the subject of journalistic balance is an extremely complex one. In 1977, at the Edinburgh Film Festival, one of the prize-winners was a film, *Before Hindsight,* which used the filmed reporting of the early days of the Hitler régime to some effect in illustrating the point that obsession with "balance" can result in extremely biased reporting if the centre-point of the so-called balance is too far to the right or the left.

In recent years, the reporting of the British Broadcasting Corporation on southern Africa has offered a good example of what many people have claimed is extensive racial bias, usually favouring the white side at the expense of the black. In fact the BBC is, of course, far more fair to both sides than is for example the politically-controlled South African Broadcasting Corporation, but the BBC's much publicized policy of "balance" in presenting controversial topics invites a close look at just how balanced its programmes on southern Africa really are. By far the greatest audience the BBC commands is that for its television services, and there are some salient points over the period 1974 to 1978 which are held by some to illustrate the BBC's own confusion in racial reporting.

There was, for instance, a 1974 American television interview with South Africa's then prime minister which the BBC later broadcast, despite the fact that even a group of white lawyers in South Africa complained that Mr Vorster's defence of apartheid was a travesty of the facts.[3] But the BBC refused to allow the other side of the matter to be put.

On 12 December of the same year BBC-2 only agreed to broadcast the anti-apartheid film *Last Grave at Dimbaza* on condition that South African government propagandists, who had already seen the film, were allowed to show their own filmed rebuttal and also appear on the programme. Significantly, the BBC later admitted in a letter that it had insisted on alterations to the anti-apartheid film, but not apparently to the pro-apartheid one (which contained a profusion of pro-apartheid half-truths and distortions, and even the falsified version of South African history set out later in Chapter 3). And seventeen days after these two films were transmitted, the BBC's director-general had a letter in a British newspaper which curiously described Mr Vorster's often false pro-apartheid statements in the interview earlier that year merely as "views", but many of *Last Grave at Dimbaza*'s anti-apartheid statements as "propaganda".

Five months later the BBC broadcast a film highly critical of the Soviet Union without any attempt at "balance" at all. Only the anti-Communist view was presented.[4] And since then the dozens of BBC filmed reports about Rhodesia have raised the comment that while there is obviously some attempt at balance, in reality most such films give the impression, to many people who have lived in southern Africa, that the viewpoint is almost wholly that of one side in the confrontation only— that of the white minority. (The film shown on 4 May 1978 being a clear case in point, featuring barely-concealed praise for the tacitly anti-black Internal Agreement, but without mentioning at all that the agreement had some serious flaws—such as the retention of most of the best land in white hands, on a basis of twenty times more land for a white than for a black—nor was any mention made of the fact that the film was made under conditions of censorship imposed by the illegal régime. Five nights later another BBC film from Rhodesia was transmitted, also subject to Rhodesian censorship but failing to mention that fact.)

This last point raises an interesting question which few members of the public are aware of, yet which the mass media are reluctant to discuss. If, as in the case of South Africa, pro-apartheid South Africans can easily travel to Britain and put their case on television and in the press, while gagging, banning and refusing passports to anti-apartheid South Africans to thus prevent them from putting *their* case through the mass media to the British public, is this not in itself a lack of balance?

The question is asked in full knowledge of the difficulties inherent in trying to balance reports from countries where the rulers censor the ruled, but the fact still remains that such rulers are only too likely to take advantage of such organizations as the BBC, which are reluctant to censor the foreign censors lest they themselves be accused of censorship. Even so, it should be noted that the BBC does today increasingly give the black viewpoint.* But the above points are mentioned because the white viewpoint is more usual. (* See end-of-chapter note.)

Where South Africa is concerned, that country adds to the general confusion of fact and fiction on racial matters by a whole series of descriptions, titles and terms which often, on examination, turn out to be the very opposite of the custom, action or law being described. The result is that if an overseas commentator merely refers to the custom or law by name, without explaining what it actually is or does, an entirely false impression—invariably favourable to apartheid—is created. Many examples can be given. Thus, the South African Extension of University Education Act sounds as if it extends the availability of university education to all South Africans. In reality, it reduced the number of universities to which blacks could be admitted, limited their ranges of course, and set up inferior "tribal colleges".

The Abolition of Passes and Co-ordination of Documents Act

abolished nothing but the right of black women *not* to have to carry a Pass. The Immorality Act does not fight immorality, but makes human love illegal and therefore allegedly immoral if between white and black. Even the state airline, South African Airways, was advertising throughout the world "South Africa? —come see for yourself" at the same time that the South African government which ran it was barring almost all black foreigners from South Africa, thus preventing most of humanity from "seeing for themselves".

Indeed, it was a black South African journalist who cuttingly commented even on the various names for South Africa's basic racial policy that "Apartheid means just 'to keep apart', but it's really anti-black discrimination. Separate Development sounds nice, but in practice means that the blacks are kept separate while the whites develop. Multi-Nationalism means the black man has his South African nationality taken from him. And Plural Democracies means single tribes in each Bantustan, with democracy nowhere to be seen."

Obviously, the gulf between how apartheid's white creators see that policy, and how the much greater number of blacks governed and controlled by it view it, could hardly be wider. Yet in this as in most other controversies, the question of which side's viewpoint is closest to the truth is most easily gauged by ignoring the rhetoric and examining the professionally documented reality instead. (Especially when the rhetoric includes such explanations as this one—given in 1977 to a BBC interviewer by a white South African MP, in answer to a question about apartheid's new face of Multi-Nationalism: "We don't call it power-sharing; we call it co-responsibility on an inter-cabinet level."[5])

Outside South Africa, there is a similar gulf. The activities of whites in Africa are often described in quite mild terms by the politicians and media of the West. Black people indulging in identical actions, however, are unthinkingly described in harsher language usually indicating disapproval. Some examples have already been given. Three more are:

1. *Kith and kin:* words used by British whites to describe their family feelings towards whites in Rhodesia. *Tribalism:* word used by British whites to describe black family feelings between blacks in Rhodesia.

2. *Settler:* a white man who has gone to live in Rhodesia. *Immigrant* : a black or brown man who has come to live in Britain—and often his children, born in Britain as well.

3. *Moderate:* a black man who is prepared to do as he is told by a white man. *Militant* : a black man who is not prepared to do as he is told by a white man. *Individualist* : a white man who is not prepared to do as he is told by anybody.

Recent European history offers other significant comparisons. When a black state in Africa strikes trouble, many newspapers are careful to mention that it *is* black. But few if any made the point that the invasion of Czechoslovakia in 1968 was by *whites*. Similarly, many newspapers of those white European nations which twice within living memory indulged in years-long orgies of mutual slaughter, claim that black wars in Africa prove that black nations "are incapable of governing themselves". One of the prime users of this argument is white South Africa—yet the last full-scale war in South Africa, from 1899 to 1902, was not between blacks and blacks, or even blacks and whites—but between whites.

In the conflicts fought by South Africa and Rhodesia in the 1970s, political motives are even applied to weapons—but again, with almost total one-sidedness.

Thus, the guerrillas fighting against white minority rule in Rhodesia have over the years had their weapons described as "Marxist", "Russian", "Iron Curtain guns", "Red Chinese bullets" and even (on 9 January 1978 in a London newspaper) as "Communist-made firearms". In South Africa in 1978, one explosion was described by the white authorities as definitely being caused by "Russian dynamite" less than ten minutes after it had gone off. Yet one never hears of "capitalist-made" firearms or dynamite.

But the other side of this coin is almost completely blank. How often do the West's mass media mention that the thousands of blacks killed by whites in southern Africa are the victims of French helicopter gun-ships, British armoured cars, American light aircraft fitted with bomb-racks, and South African bombs, grenades, shells, bullets and napalm? Not to mention British and French jet aircraft?

This technique of what is known as "responsibility-shift" is of course by no means confined to the reportage of affairs in southern Africa. One can see it in reports from most parts of the world where there is conflict, and where the West has already taken sides. But in the case of South Africa, for instance, the mass media in Britain, particularly, has a tendency to make excuses for white South Africans while laying the blame for apartheid, prison torture, the invasion of Angola, the Department of Information scandal and almost every other indefensible policy and action, on the South African government. Yet that government holds power because white South Africans in the November 1977 whites-only general election (and every election since 1948) voted it into power by a majority of the votes of whites—and actually gave it a record 82 per cent of seats in 1977, the first election after the Soweto riots in which, to quote official mortuary records, 60 per cent of the dozens of unarmed black children killed by the white police were shot in the back or the side.

There is no doubt that this particular responsibility-shift is a function of race. But what is really meant by "race"? Interestingly, the authorities on that subject, the anthropologists, are cautious. Within each "race", they say, there are often wider overall differences than there are between the various racial groups themselves, and in any case it is the general opinion of anthropologists that there is no such thing as a "pure" race. So it has been truly said that those who make the greatest noise about racial differences in their community are by definition those who know least about the subject.

To most white people, however, a rough-and-ready definition of what they mean by someone of a different race would be a person whose coloration is genetically different from their own, to an extent that is inheritable, and who exhibits a temperamental/cultural variation from the white norm.

Unfortunately for the world's white racists, this happens to include red-haired white people. Their coloration is certainly different—they can be spotted as "different" at a distance—and their skin, unlike that of other whites, will not suntan. The difference is genetic and can be passed on to children. And the general belief that redheads are genetically violent-tempered and excitable has quite as much validity as the belief that blacks are genetically musical. At least in Britain, there can also be differences in the redheads' culture and speech, as a fair proportion of them happen to be Scottish.

Since by the racists' own definitions redheads are therefore a different race, all one now has to do is to apply the racists' solutions of various race "problems" to redheads, and the rationality and validity of such solutions can be instantly gauged.

In South Africa, for instance, there should be a Redheads' Homeland, or "Redheadstan". The Mixed Marriages and Immorality Act should be extended to stop redheads from inter-breeding with—or even kissing—whites with blonde, brown or black hair. A special Redhead Division should be created within the South African Department for Plural Relations. Tests for redheadedness should be devised by the South African Race Classification Board in Pretoria. And redheads should be instantly barred from owning property in "white" South Africa, entering white restaurants and hotels, occupying public office, and exercising the vote. Simply because they are redheads.

In Britain, the necessary adjustments need not be so drastic, but the newspapers and politicians should immediately make the public aware of the "redhead problem", parents should com-plain about unfair proportions of redheads in their children's school classes, and redheads should be pointed out in the street and muttered about by the racially prejudiced. For after all redheads are, by public definition, a "different" race, and should by that illogical definition be treated as such.

Perhaps only two more points need be made on this subject of race, as defined by those who take it on themselves to con-tinually stress that other human beings are racially different from themselves, and so must be treated differently.

The first concerns the highly emotional subject of IQ and its relation to skin colour, with some academics claiming "the whiter, the brighter". Others, however, are now pointing out that equally valid research suggests that blacks exhibit less collective aggressiveness than whites, so that in this nuclear age an all-black world would be rather less likely to destroy all life on earth in a nuclear war than an all-white world. Which race, therefore, is truly the most intelligent?

The second point concerning the effects of obsession with racial differences was made in Germany 22 years after the end of World War II, by someone who knows better than most people where such obsessions can finally lead.

Referring to millions of people of "non-Aryan" races murdered by Nazi Germany between 1933 and 1945, Dr Albert

Rueckerl, Director of the West German Central Agency for the Prosecution of Nazi Criminals, said: "The dreadful number of dead is not even the point. It is the basic insanity of categorizing humanity that matters."[6]

This is the crux of the matter, and it destroys the most popular of all those many arguments used by South Africa's apologists in the West, the claim that South African apartheid is no worse—and possibly a good deal better—than other forms of tyranny, such as communism. For this argument, which has been used even by some of the West's leading statesmen, is a classic *non-sequitur*. It is as illogical in its own way as the Communist argument that because Russia has elections, then Russia is quite as democratic as America. For it pretends that two entirely different concepts are one and the same.

It was the late Chief Albert Luthuli of the African National Congress, South Africa's only Nobel Peace Prize winner, who some twenty years ago put the whole subject into perspective with brevity and logic. He warned that people should not deceive themselves into thinking that racism was just another tyranny like political tyranny or religious tyranny. "I know of many men who have changed their politics, and many who have changed their religion," he said. "But I have never known a man who could change his race. And that is why racism is the path to Armageddon for humanity. For racism is the only *absolute* tyranny."

It is a rather obvious truth—but most opinion-influencers in the West have still to grasp it, much less its equally obvious implications. Thus, to keep out of trouble, the average oppressed worker in a Communist country merely has to keep his mouth shut. But how does a black South African hide the colour of his skin? And the difference between racial tyranny and political tyranny goes even further than that. The Communist worker with talent can rise to the very highest positions in the country in which he was born. The talented black worker of South African birth cannot, solely because of something irrelevant to his abilities and entirely beyond his control—his skin colour. (The point is important, and is expanded on in Chapter 8.)

Racial tyranny such as apartheid is therefore in a wholly different class from other tyrannies, which depend on beliefs or views held by individuals. And in South Africa, the fact that the whole control structure depends on a flexible divide-and-rule classification based solely on major and minor racial variations was clearly shown by the Africa Bureau of London in a report in 1978 :

The following table shows the variety of permutations by which the population of South Africa is divided to suit the white minority's purposes.

Division	Which Groups	Official Functions
1 nation	All	control by security apparatus
2 nations	White/Non-White or Bantu/Non-Bantu	virtually all public amenities, sex, marriage, public transport, tax, influx control
3 nations	White; Coloured/Indian; Bantu	statutory race groups, film censorship, parties, trades unions, official wage hierarchy
4 nations	Whites; Coloured; Asiatic; Bantu	Government race ministries, some census statistics, some job reservation decrees
5 nations	White; Coloured; Indian; Chinese; Bantu	beaches, all group areas outside the Cape Colony
6 nations	White; Coloured; Indian; Chinese; Cape Malay; Bantu	group areas legislation—defining residence rights
11 nations	White English; White Afrikaans; Coloured; Asian; seven Bantu nations	ethnic groups officially recognized for schools and radio
11 nations (alternative divide)	White; Coloured; Indian; eight "Bantu National Units"	groups for which segregated political structures have been erected

Division	Which Groups	Official Functions
13 nations	White; Coloured; Indian; Chinese; Malay; eight "Bantu National units"	total residential segregation, including "ethnic" zoning in black "locations"
18 nations	White English; White Afrikaans; Cape Coloured; Other Coloured; Cape Malay; Griqua; Chinese; Indians; Other Asiatic; N. Sotho; S. Sotho; Swazi; Tsonga; Tswana; Venda; Xhosa (Ciskei); Xhosa (Transkei); Zulu	total number of official ethnic groups recognized by statute and proclamation includes nine "Bantu National Units" and seven Coloured sub groups

This leads to a further aspect of the realities of racism in South Africa which again seems to have escaped the attention of the West's policy-makers. There is a somewhat cynical catch-phrase in English-speaking countries: "If you can't beat them, join them". If all else fails, give in, accept defeat and join forces with your enemy. At least you might be able to change the system from within. But South Africa is the only country in the world where this final escape from oppression cannot apply.

For apartheid ensures that blacks are always separate from whites, and so cannot join them. Even the limited escape route offered by most old-fashioned aristocracies—the nobleman marrying the commoner—is barred to black South Africans under the Mixed Marriages, Immorality and other Acts of apartheid. The black South African is therefore permanently denied the ultimate escape of "joining them". And so the only possible way out is to "beat them". In short, the white South African minority appears to have so structured its race laws that the only possible escape from oppression for the black majority is to destroy white South Africa, totally and permanently.

Yet this black majority is the subject of yet another series of misconceptions in the West, for it is neither as primitive nor as savage as popular opinion throught the white world often makes out. The source-societies from which modern black South Africa arose were, in their own way, a microcosm of latter-day Europe. Some were peaceful, some warlike—although not even the feared black Moselekatse of the early nineteenth century ever plumbed the depths of the white Stalin or Hitler. Most pre-white black societies were stable and well-ordered, and they ate well and did not suffer especially from disease.

The white man largely destroyed these black societies, which were forced to re-form in ways which today often represent a mingling of white and black cultures—perhaps most easily seen in the black customs and white beliefs of many modern black churches in South Africa. At the same time the fragmentation of communities and the splitting up of black families to conform to the rigid categories and mass population evictions demanded by the apartheid master-plan has left a substantial section of black South Africa rootless, bewildered and with its indigenous culture destroyed and already half-forgotten. It is a point worth remembering when white propagandists attempt to make political capital out of the often apathetic nature of black South Africans, both as individuals and in the mass—for much the same apathy and bewilderment could be seen in the 1940s on the faces of the millions of white refugees and displaced persons who owed their plight to the activities of another nationalist state based on the concept of white racial purity.

Whether it is fair and reasonable to make such comparisons is the subject of a later chapter. This one has attempted to sketch out in broad perspective the usually unconscious racial bias in the white West against which the activities of South Africa's racial propaganda can be seen in clearer perspective, and to fill in some of the facts—although some might describe these only as opinions—of race, racial prejudice and racial misunderstanding.

Perhaps "opinions" is the better word. The dividing-line between the many human characteristics due to culture, and those due to race, is at times so indistinct that much more experienced writers than the present author have at times stumbled over them.

There is, too, the difficulty most of the West's white people have of developing any kind of empathetic understanding of the attitudes, history and viewpoints of the black peoples of southern Africa. It is because of this that certain analogies are drawn throughout this book, in the hope of clearer insights across the barriers of race and culture. For to establish that distortions of the truth have taken place in the images of southern Africa presented by the white minorities' propaganda is one thing. To bring into satisfactorily sharp focus the racial truths that have thus been long concealed is quite another.

* Defenders of the BBC can rightly point to fair reports such as producer Jenny Barraclough's "Portrait of a 'Terrorist' ", featuring Robert Mugabe (BBC-2, April 1979), as genuine racial balance. (See page 33.)

CHAPTER TWO

The South African Propaganda Machine

"Propaganda is neither more nor less than a weapon—but a really terrible one in the hands of one who understands it.... The task of propaganda is to unite, and the task of the united is propaganda."

ADOLF HITLER, *Mein Kampf.*

IN APRIL, 1978, the world at large first became aware of the existence of a huge and lavishly financed propaganda organization operated by the whites-only South African government. In that month, in order to explain large discrepancies in government funding, the South African Department of Information handed in a letter admitting certain facts to an official investigating committee. This letter stated that public moneys had in fact been appropriated for the purpose of bribing foreign journalists to write favourable articles about the new showpiece of apartheid, the allegedly autonomous and self-governing Transkei black "homeland", for the political manipulation of certain African states in the hope of fostering divisive factions within the Organization of African Unity, and for giving free, all-expenses-paid working holidays in South Africa to right-wing foreign newsmen who could be expected to write articles in defence of apartheid.

The political manoeuvring and so-called scandals surrounding these revelations were seized on by the world's media to the almost total exclusion of the implications of these events for South Africa's integrity, trustworthiness and true racial and political character. Scapegoats were eventually marked out and dismissed, the disgraced Department of Information was officially disbanded—to be instantly replaced by a remarkably similar organization called the Bureau of Internal and International Communications, the cracks were papered over and the South African press (and foreign newsmen in South Africa) was actively discouraged from further investigation. But the cosmetic operation was short-lived.

In late October 1978, even greater scandals involving the Department of Information were exposed in South Africa. A Supreme Court judge, Mr Justice Anton Mostert, had been investigating contraventions of South Africa's strict exchange control regulations. Some of the sworn evidence given to him suggested extensive misappropriation of public funds by the Department of Information. The judge ignored an urgent request by the South African Prime Minister, Mr P. Botha, to keep silent on the matter and publicly stated that there were "indications of corruption—in the wider sense of the word—relating to public funds".

This particular story had begun three years earlier, when a wealthy, pro-apartheid Afrikaner businessman had attempted to buy South African Associated Newspapers, owners of most of South Africa's anti-apartheid and anti-government press. If the attempt had succeeded, almost all South African newspapers would have been pro-government. But it failed, and instead the businessman, with at least £7 million of ready capital behind him, set up a new English-language newspaper, *The Citizen*, strongly pro-government and frequently boasting of its success in taking readership away from the anti-government *Rand Daily Mail*, part of the South African Associated Newspapers group.

Detailed, sworn evidence before Judge Mostert in October 1978 stated that the millions of pounds used first in the attempt to buy South African Associated Newspapers, and then in setting up *The Citizen*, were public funds misappropriated by the Department of Information and supplied by devious means to the Afrikaner businessman.

In the event, there is no doubt that *The Citizen*'s pro-government propaganda helped swing much non-Afrikaner white support behind the government at the 1977 general election, at which it won unprecedented support. And further evidence sworn in front of Judge Mostert claimed that £6 million had also been allocated by the South African government's propaganda machine for the intended purchase by a friendly American businessman of an influential American newspaper, which would then quietly infiltrate the propaganda of the South African government into America.

By the end of October, public demands were being made in South Africa for an open enquiry to establish all the facts. But the prime minister, Pieter Botha, refused to agree to any enquiry. Three days later, he was forced to change his mind, agreed to a Commission of Enquiry and announced that the whole affair was now *sub judice*. This was seen as an attempt to cover up, especially since the London *Times* pointed out that the evidence "showed that some of the most important members of the South African government were involved", and named Mr Vorster, the former prime minister, Dr C. Mulder, Minister of Information, and General Hendrik van den Bergh, former head of the Bureau of State Security (BOSS), who had been appointed by Mr Vorster earlier in 1978 to look into the April scandal of the Information Department for the government. In the meantime, the *Rand Daily Mail* had described the unfolding affair as "exceeding even the scandal of Watergate".

On 7 November, Dr Mulder resigned his post as information minister, stating "I have no pangs of conscience because everything I have done I did in the conviction that I was serving my country". The businessman who had bought *The Citizen* similarly said that his actions could be explained "because it was for my country".

Also on 7 November, Prime Minister Botha sacked Judge Mostert, and ordered him to conduct no further enquiries. On the following day, government officials successfully applied to the Supreme Court in Pretoria for an interdict to prevent Judge Mostert addressing a press conference that afternoon. On the same day the prime minister threatened to introduce press censorship into South Africa.

On 12 November, Judge Mostert's home was the target of a petrol bomb attack, but the unknown assailant bombed the house next door by mistake.

Ten days later, there was a further important development. The Foreign Affairs Association of South Africa, a quasi-academic body claiming to be an impartial observer and interpreter of the South African political and racial scene in the international context, announced it was disbanding. The anti-government press in South Africa had uncovered evidence that the association was not independent, but had received 75 per cent of its total funding from the government of South Africa. This opened up a particularly interesting new facet, because again, the South African government's official propaganda machine was mentioned in connection with these new revelations, and the FAA had been responsible for inviting hundreds of influential overseas politicians and opinion-formers to South Africa, including Dr Kissinger himself, who spoke highly of the Association.

Again, further interesting links were established by press investigations. Four of the five known sponsors of one of South Africa's most vociferous independent lobbying organizations overseas, including the Afrikaner businessman behind *The Citizen*, were found to have served on the FAA board as trustees. And the South African opposition press commented that it seemed likely that up to 130 allegedly private and independent South African "information" and "international" groups would eventually be found to have been funded in some form or another by apartheid's propaganda machine, the South African Department of Information, and were in reality "front" organizations for the government, energetically spreading that government's propaganda distortions and untruths throughout the world under the guise of "factual" information spread by "impartial private sources".

By mid-December 1978 a government commission had revealed that at last count there were at least some 138 secret, government-funded "fifth column" propaganda organizations, of which no less than 68 were to remain secret and continue their task of infiltrating and slanting the world's information services on behalf of the creators of apartheid. Or in South Africa's own words, they were to penetrate "hostile" foreign newspapers, and engage in media manipulation throughout the world. Also revealed was the so-called "American strategy", in which skilled South African government propagandists attempted (often with substantial success) to subvert senior US officials in Washington by direct contact.

By this time, it was public knowledge that the attempt to turn a respected American newspaper into a disguised propaganda agent of the South African government was but a small part of a vast plan for the wholesale, secretive subversion of entire media groups of magazines, newspapers and television services all over the world, using South African government money. Several of the private South African businessmen thus involved confessed their part in an exercise to use such money to take over one of Europe's most influential magazine groups. Attempts were even made to surreptitiously "buy" British magazines produced by and for coloured people in Britain, and in Africa.

Tapes recorded by Dr Eschel Rhoodie (the dismissed head of the Information Department) then occupied the limelight. Amidst warnings by two of the people involved, that a full exposure of South Africa's worldwide activities would have "disastrous consequences for South Africa diplomatically, economically and politically", it became known that South African arms and propaganda manipulation had even been involved in lengthening Nigeria's bloody Biafran civil war; and that in a hostile act against the United Nations itself, South Africa had been operating a ship-borne radio station off the Namibian coast and broadcasting fake SWAPO guerrilla programmes in order to embarrass the U.N., whose responsibility Namibia properly is. Indeed, as it rumbles on, the scandal produces more and more evidence that no act, however reprehensible, was apparently considered too extreme in attacking apartheid's critics and in spreading apartheid's divisive propaganda. But what that propaganda actually says, the world's media has been oddly silent about. A strange omission which this book attempts to repair in some detail, for it does seem that the nature of racial misinformation can be just as important as how it is spread.

It may be years before this, the greatest known exercise in planned international deception, is fully and finally uncovered. But within five weeks of its first exposure, the whitewashing exercise of closing government ranks and blaming everything on one or two "misguided" people had already begun—with the announcement of Prime Minister Botha that his cabinet could not "be held responsible for the misdeeds of just one minister".

But in fact, as will be seen in detail later in this chapter, almost the entire South African white nation is the real propaganda machine—not just the ephemeral Department of Information. Even during the above revelations, the same propaganda books with the same untruthful racial statements and arguments were still being handed out by the South African embassies and fellow-traveller organizations throughout the West. The same cabinet ministers were giving the same propagandist, pro-apartheid speeches. The same South African media manipulation and public-relations activities were continuing almost unabated. And this author even received an impolite letter from the director of a well-known South African (white) Chamber of Commerce, accusing him of being untruthful, yet containing one of the standard Department of Information falsehoods about black wages (ironically revealed as a falsehood by Bureau of Statistics figures included with the letter), claiming a "narrowing" of the black/white wage gap (see page 114) when it had actually widened.

The pretence that all South African misinformation was the fault of a handful of Department of Information officials, and that now that they have been dismissed everything is "normal", is one that is already being energetically broadcast throughout the world. This chapter reveals how much real reliance can be placed on it. But perhaps an account by Bishop Ambrose Reeves, once Bishop of Johannesburg, as to what Mr Vorster actually said in 1975 to President Tolbert of Liberia in "explanation" of apartheid gives a hint as to the real sources of South African propaganda.

Briefly, Mr Vorster told the Liberian president that Bantustan chiefs were all elected by their people. This is untrue. All of them—Chiefs Matanzima, Mangope, Ntsanwisi and so on— were either nominated (often by the South African government itself) or were in "homelands" that had never had an election.

Mr Vorster said "influx control" in South Africa was not discrimination, but a practical policy to prevent an evil. But the policy applies only to black South Africans, not whites, Coloureds or Asians.

On education, Mr Vorster told President Tolbert that the standard in all schools was the same. He did not mention the fifteen-to-one bias in favour of white children in the allocation of educational funds in South Africa.

Mr Vorster even said that there were no political detainees in South Africa—yet laws in which he was involved as Minister of Justice apply stringent restrictions only against political prisoners (such as denial of any news of the outside world), and these restrictions were being applied against dozens of prisoners at the time. (*The Times*, London, 25/2/75.)

These are all standard South African propaganda themes as spread by the Department of Information. That more than just that department has in fact been involved in spreading them can also be seen by three brief examples of their effect in America and Europe.

In the US, in 1971/72, the Nixon administration opted for the so-called "Tar Baby" option as official US policy towards South Africa. Yet this option, calling for a particularly soft line on South Africa, contained as its "factual" rationale most of the major—and untrue—South African propaganda themes about race, economics and South Africa's "total" loyalty to the free world, detailed here in later pages.

In Britain, in April 1970, the Conservative Party produced a policy report on the British use of the contentious Simonstown naval base near Cape Town. A comparison between this report and an article on the same subject in the South African London embassy's propaganda magazine *Report from South Africa* of December 1969 shows the two to be curiously similar. And in 1979, a European Parliament report on South Africa's racial employment practices was found to be heavily loaded with apartheid propaganda, and was rejected.

There are other aspects to this basing of some Western foreign policies towards South Africa on arguments of South African origin. For coupled with the unparalleled flood of "information" from South Africa, is an effective, long-term operation within that country to gag and silence the voice of apartheid's critics by bannings, threats, censorship, the withholding of passports and indefinite imprisonment without trial, so that by mid-1978 the Johannesburg *Star* was able to print the names of more than 1,000 critics of the government thus silenced, without trial and often without even explanation.

White South Africa, the sole source of South African racial and other propaganda, consists of little more than four million men, women and children. By comparison, Britain has a population of roughly 50 million, Russia 250 million, India 600 million and China 850 million. But in the 1970s, an American newspaper editor complained, "I receive more propaganda from South Africa than from *all* other countries combined".[1]

What is propaganda? Basically, it is the propagation of a belief or doctrine. More commonly today, it is a series of claims and arguments intended to bias the recipient towards the views of the propagandist. In the case of totalitarian states, however,

it can often—as Adolf Hitler has noted—be a complex of multi-
media and public-relations persuasion and indoctrination
aimed at creating an "image" of a country and/or policy which
may actually be the very opposite of the truth, but which
always serves only the interests of the state.

Depending on the circumstances under which it is introduced,
and the beliefs it is intended to inculcate, propaganda can be
extremely dangerous to a society into which it is introduced.
In his book *Guns or Butter?* (Putnam, 1938) the British
journalist/diplomat Bruce Lockhart noted of German propaganda on racial matters: "Today, largely on account of
Germany's attitude, anti-semitism has become one of the
gravest problems in the civilised world. . . . It is raising its ugly
head in countries where it was previously unknown. . . ." Is it
entirely wrong to suggest that this statement still has at least
some validity today if one simply changes "Germany" to "South
Africa" and "anti-semitism" to "white racial prejudice"?

The dangers of divisive propaganda based on half-truths and
untruths can be seen perhaps most clearly by reducing it to the
personal level. For instance, what propaganda actually does is
to distort one's vision of reality—as if one were wearing a faulty
pair of spectacles, through which a hole in the road might
appear as a harmless shadow and be walked into with unpleasant
consequences—as both Britain and America have discovered
with Rhodesia.

More specifically, South Africa's statistical distortion of the
real size of the income gap between black and white (see Chapter
Four) is not unlike a shrewd businessman persuading others to
invest in him by his claim of good employer/employee relations
—when in fact his employees are boiling with discontent. South
Africa's propaganda half-truths and omissions about its rôle—
both anti-Nazi and pro-Nazi—in World War II (Chapter 6),
in the hope of acceptance as a military ally by the West, is
perhaps not so different from a firm appointing as a security
guard a man who has hidden a record of gross disloyalty to his
previous employers.

And perhaps even more to the point, South Africa's often
successful propaganda for the alleged justice and "acceptance
by all races" of its apartheid policies could possibly be likened
to a farmer trying to persuade his neighbours to adopt a radical
new method of gaining his farm-labourers' hard work and co-

operation—without mentioning that the system can only be made to work at the point of a gun.

To fully describe the ramifications, methods, successes and dangers of South Africa's racial-propaganda machine would take several volumes. In line with the general theme of this book, then, attention will instead be focused on those aspects of propaganda, and of South Africa's use of it, which are relatively or completely unsuspected. And perhaps the briefest way to begin is to list the main methods by which facts are altered, inverted and avoided by the professional propagandist in a major campaign; specifically, those of South Africa.

SOUTH AFRICAN PROPAGANDA TECHNIQUES

In the skilled science of propaganda—as in any other science—certain recognized techniques exist. These can be used to change truth into untruth, introduce significant bias, undermine criticism so as to at least temporarily discredit critics, and consistently evade trenchant issues by the liberal use of *non-sequiturs* and red herrings. As noted later, propaganda was first handled in this precise manner on a large scale by Dr Goebbels and other leading Nazi propagandists, and there is an undoubted similarity between pre-war Nazi propaganda and modern South African propaganda. However, with the rise since the war of sophisticated advertising and public-relations research, publicity and persuasion techniques, South African propaganda today is often so carefully constructed as to be unrecognizable as propaganda at all, and detection techniques such as that of Error Bias, explained later in this chapter, may be necessary in order to disentangle fact from fiction.

Generally speaking, all propaganda is a mixture of some or all of the following techniques of deception, to which recent South African examples will be added in explanation.

Untruths

In effective, well-constructed propaganda, the outright untruth is only used where strictly necessary, as public exposure of a clear untruth casts serious doubt on the rest of the propaganda. However, the most important use of the outright untruth is usually as the basis of a long and shrewdly argued propaganda theme of such complexity that even those who are suspicious of it tend to get embroiled in details before they reach the basic untruth at the core of the whole scheme. As discussed at some length in the next chapter, South Africa's Bantustan policy is an excellent example of this. So many critics of apartheid have spent so much time arguing the morality of the end-product— Bantustans or "black homelands"—that none of the more prominent figures in the debate has ever realized that the basic historical foundation of the policy is almost pure fiction. Once this major deceit is exposed, both the Bantustan policy and the credibility of its creators and propagandists begin to crumble away.

Half-truths

These are by far the most common form of deception, largely because they can produce a misinformation effect just as great as that of a deliberate untruth—yet without necessarily discrediting the propagandist when he is found out. Thus it is true, as South Africa claims, that the Transkei "homeland" is the size of Wales. It is true that only about 2 per cent or 3 per cent of black South Africans are affected by Job Reservation determinations. It is true that South African troops fought loyally for the free world in World War II. But it is also true that Adolf Hitler built some very good roads and was fond of children, and that most Russians live much better under communism than they did under capitalism. The half-truth, in other words, depends on frequent repetition of usually irrelevant facts, coupled with suppression of the really relevant facts. And the relevant facts that have been suppressed in the examples given above for South Africa are that the Transkei is also only one-thirtieth the size of South Africa (for one-fifth of South Africa's people); that only about 2 per cent or 3 per cent of black South Africans are allowed to do the same job as whites, almost all the rest doing inferior jobs; and that the political party which now rules South Africa was largely pro-Nazi in World War II.

Omissions

This aspect of propaganda is particularly characteristic of the often impressive reference works published in South Africa. What is probably the largest and best-known of these simply leaves out such important—but revealing—aspects of South African life as the powerful, furtive Broederbond (which it does not even mention in passing). For years, its editions eulogized South African skills at soccer without once mentioning that the all-white soccer body it praised had for years been excluded from international sport for racial bias, nor did it even hint that the non-racial body which the world does recognize, was automatically refused passports by the all-white South African government. This is one of the many propaganda methods which to the ordinary enquirer offers no evidence of its existence. (Admittedly, the massive bias which this method introduces into even the most apparently innocent reference work or official document, is usually quickly apparent to enquirers who know something already of the broad facts of the situation—but they are less likely to need the reference book.) And there is, of course, a hidden censorship factor at work in all such books published in South Africa, which they always fail to mention. This is that many of the opponents of the South African government's race policies may not be quoted, or sometimes even mentioned, in material published in South Africa. Thus, all South African-published works touching on politics or race are by definition pre-biased towards the white pro-apartheid view, the real anti-apartheid view being censored out, in effect.

Red herrings
The greatest red herring in South African material is the "Communist threat". This is trailed across everything from the Soweto uprising of 1976 to protests by Catholic priests about the infamies of apartheid. The setting up of false trails is a favourite occupation of the skilled propagandist, and many is the famous politician of the free world who is to be seen doggedly following such trails to the often total exclusion of the relevant facts.

Non-sequiturs
This is the simple and effective technique of giving a perfectly plausible answer to a question which has never been asked, instead of answering the question which has been asked. In the South African context, overseas observers who ask how black South African incomes compare with white South African in-comes are instead told how they compare with black Congolese,

Malawian or Ugandan incomes, or even with incomes in Hong Kong. Enquirers who ask in South Africa about the actual disparity between white and black education expenditures are likely instead to be taken on a tour of a few selected "show" schools for Africans near Johannesburg or Pretoria. And so on. The cure for the *non-sequitur* is to keep asking the original question.

The "horse's mouth"

In countries such as South Africa where government control of the oppressed sector of the community is total, pressure can easily be brought to bear on members of the oppressed community to repeat government propaganda claims as if they are true. Thus, one finds even educated black South Africans endorsing the government's false version of South African history, and blaming the enslavement of the black majority not on the Afrikaner Nationalists, but "on the Englishmen"—to quote one such black on British television.

These are the basic techniques available to the determined propagandist. One could perhaps add False Comparisons and False Analogies, but they are more correctly classed as methods of using some of the techniques listed above. What should be mentioned, however, is that the really skilled propagandist can consistently produce a wholly false impression without actually writing or uttering any identifiable falsehoods. The point is important because this technique is one of the most powerful defences available to a professional propagandist. He can simply challenge his critics to point to any false statements to back up their criticisms of his claim, which they will be unable to do.

But there is, nevertheless, a simple technique which quickly exposes all kinds of propaganda—even the most shrewd. It is called Error Bias. Its one disadvantage is that those applying it must be well acquainted with the subject under discussion, yet even moderate—but accurate—knowledge is usually sufficient to apply it as a test of the veracity of any propaganda theme.

Error Bias rests on the observation that in any given set of general information, there are likely to be some errors of fact. If there is more than a bare minimum of these errors, then the source of the information is either inexpert or careless, or is propagandist or has been exposed to propaganda. Which of these two explanations is correct—the carelessly inaccurate or the deliberately biased—can be ascertained very quickly by the simple method of listing all the errors (distortions, *non-sequiturs*, omissions, untruths) in two columns, "pro" the argument, and "con". If all or nearly all the errors fall into one column, then the suspect information is in fact propaganda.

In most cases of South African propaganda, the method works particularly well because the "pro" and "con" aspects of the information can usually be related directly to racial matters. To give a brief, but actual example of information given to a British VIP during a visit to South Africa, one can probably do little better than to quote from a talk about that country given to the Regent Advertising Club in London by the late Sir Thomas Blackburn, Chairman of the Beaverbrook group of newspapers in Britain. The contents of this talk are significant for two reasons. The first is that, as head of one of Britain's largest and best-known mass media organizations, "Tom" Blackburn could be expected to wield some influence on the type of information about South Africa appearing in his group's newspapers. The second is that Tom Blackburn was an honest man, who apparently believed that certain other people were equally honest.

After a lavish lunch at the South African embassy shortly after his return from his tour of that country, this is an extract from what he told the Regent Advertising Club. The Error Bias of the information he was given in South Africa is noted in parenthesis.

"Blacks and whites", said Sir Thomas, "arrived in South Africa at about the same time." (Pro-apartheid untruth.) "The Bantustans are irrevocable," (pro-apartheid untruth—sections of them such as the Blyde River Canyon scenic reserve had already been revoked). "Apartheid in the cities only means that blacks and whites, who have mingled at work, go back to their own suburbs at night, just as I go back to my own suburb in London." (Pro-apartheid distortion: the black Johannes-burgers are forced by law to live in Soweto, but Sir Thomas could live where he wished.)

"South Africa is not a multi-racial society, but a multi-national one." (Pro-apartheid distortion; the "nations" in South Africa are simply the different races.) "The black people are a very happy lot." (Pro-apartheid distortion.) "The black man prefers apartheid." (Pro-apartheid untruth, verified as untrue two years later in a poll.) "The black man does not wish to mix with whites." (Pro-apartheid untruth.)

"The South African Coloureds arose only from Hottentots, Bushmen and foreign sailors." (Pro-Afrikaner untruth, invented to pretend that no Afrikaners interbred with non-whites.) "The United Nations is just a propaganda platform." (Pro-government distortion.) "I have been told by Mr Vorster that Mrs Helen Joseph (of house-arrest fame) is a Communist." (Pro-government smear; Mrs Joseph is an anti-Communist Christian.) "Go to South Africa and see it all for yourselves." (Pro-apartheid distortion; only whites could then visit South Africa, and several members of his audience were coloured.)

With eleven errors biased towards apartheid and its creators, and none towards the other side, the mathematical probability that Tom Blackburn's talk was (unwitting) propaganda for apartheid works out at at least a thousand to one. In fact, the probability is far higher when one notes that almost all the pro-apartheid errors faithfully mirror South African government propaganda untruths and distortions, as found in government publications and spread by government officials.

However, those sufficiently interested in this subject of propaganda detection are advised not to take the above example for granted, but to test for Error Bias themselves. There are large numbers of statements, speeches and apologias made about South Africa every year, in most Western countries, by a variety of people and organizations, from politicians to banks and industrial groups with investments in South Africa. The reasonably well-informed researcher into South African affairs is therefore invited to test the efficiency of the Error Bias detection technique by actually using it. The results are often very interesting indeed.

(Where racial propaganda is concerned there is, as touched on elsewhere in this book, another detection technique known as Substitution, where one simply substitutes "white" for "black" and vice versa. The result is often to expose apparently innocuous statements as clearly racist in character.)

SOUTH AFRICA'S RACIAL PROPAGANDA ORGANIZATIONS

The means by which South African propaganda is both broadcast to the world and infiltrated into the corridors of power in a surprisingly large number of nations—including some black ones—may be without parallel in its size and scope in human history. And when one realizes that this massive exercise is undertaken by and on behalf of a mere four million or so whites at the southern tip of Africa, representing barely one-thousandth of the world's population, the whole operation appears even more extraordinary. Yet it exists and it exerts a profound and usually quite unsuspected influence on world politics and business decisions, for reasons now being increasingly unmasked.

At the heart of this giant effort was the South African Department of Information, which vied with the Department of Foreign Affairs as the most important government ministry in South Africa. Thirty years ago, its budget was about R50,000 per annum. By 1978 it was more than one hundred times that amount—rising to R5 million in 1968 and some R16 million in 1978. The department occupied large, modern premises in Pretoria, completely equipped with the latest audio-visual and research facilities. It employed directly many hundreds of people—almost all of them white—and it drew on the skills and overseas contacts of many of South Africa's leading advertising and public relations companies. It was—and with a new face, probably still is—one of the best financed and most efficient of all the persuasion-industries in the world today.

This, however, is only the tip of the iceberg. Ranged beneath the South African government's still-extant propaganda system is a wide variety of organizations, media, publishing houses and lobbying systems either directly or indirectly engaged in spreading and supporting the South African's government's main propaganda themes and current campaigns of persuasion.

The use of the word "campaigns" is deliberate, for several professional advertising people have noted that South African racial propaganda is invariably underscored by specific themes and catch-phrases, and is possibly unique in this respect. The best-known of these carefully-orchestrated themes are probably : "Separate Development of the races," "Multi-national," "*verligte* and *verkrampte*," "Dialogue," "Détente," "Bastion of the West against communism," and "black homelands policy". Such slogans eventually become "shorthand" for propaganda ploys which are not necessarily true at all.

Yet these are the very techniques, not of the professional

government information official, but of the commercial adver-
tiser with a very large budget. As each theme begins to lose its
power, another is created to take its place. And the whole
expensive operation of campaign after campaign is monitored
and adjusted by the very kind of professional market-research
operation that the South African Department of Information
was, in 1973, found to be engaged in on a worldwide basis.

In that year, a professional attitude-survey was conducted
in fourteen countries throughout the world by an American
research group. The official South African interest in the survey
was disguised by asking questions of a wide variety of people
about their attitudes to many countries and political policies
throughout the world, of which South Africa was only one. In
October 1974 the South African Minister of Information
explained to parliament in Cape Town that "we have now
gone over to the offensive. We are now equipped with an area
map, so to speak, on which we can intelligently base our
strategy; a map showing enemy strengths and weaknesses."

It is, of course, perfectly legitimate for a country to use
modern attitude surveys and advertising techniques to put its
own point of view. But how reflective of genuine realities in
South Africa have been the long procession of professionally-
mounted campaigns of persuasion, from "separate development"
through "South Africa needs more time" to "plural democracies"? One example, carefully studied at the time, perhaps gives
a hint of the whole.

Of all these various efforts to improve South Africa's image
throughout the world, perhaps the *verligte*-vs.-*verkrampte*
exercise offers the best opportunity for contrasting the promises
made with the actions—if any—actually taken to fulfil those
promises. This is possible because several agencies actually
monitor the South African press and daily political realities
year by year in order to detect any real signs of a basic change
in government racial policies.

The *verligtes* and the *verkramptes* made their main début
through the world's press and South African publicity sources
in 1967. (*Verlig* means "enlightened"; *verkramp* means
"bigoted"). By 1968 they were a major talking-point whenever
South Africa was mentioned, and critics of apartheid were
frequently admonished that the *verlig* Afrikaner Nationalists
were indulging in a "vigorous debate" within the South African

power structure, the outcome of which would be a clear victory for liberal enlightenment if only the outside world would "have patience". Even the august London *Times* devoted a special leading article to applauding the whole *verligte* concept. But amongst all the millions of words, what did the *verligtes* actually *do* that was enlightened?

There was a great deal that they could have done. For instance, they could at least have raised their voices when, shortly after their emergence, their government created the Terrorism Act—providing for unlimited imprisonment without trial—and applied it also to the UN territory of Namibia. But the *verligtes* did nothing and kept silent.

In July 1968 the main Afrikaner church launched a campaign for the immediate suppression of the teaching of the theory of evolution in South African schools and universities. The *verligtes* did nothing. In 1968, too, 35 black Namibians were illegally tried in Pretoria, and the International Commission of Jurists commented that the trial proved the "reality of prison torture" in South Africa. The *verligtes* ignored the whole affair.

In mid-1969, a white South African automobile club took over another local motoring group and threw out its existing Coloured members. The *verligtes* looked the other way. In July 1968, a British newspaper produced documentary and photographic proof of excessively cruel child-labour practices for black children on white South African farms. The *verligtes* kept silent —as they had earlier in the year when adult blacks were told of new government laws turning them into migrant labour in their own country. And late in 1968, when the all-Afrikaner Pretoria City Council refused a request for black charities to collect money in Pretoria, re-affirming that only white charities would have that right, not a *verligte* raised his voice in protest. Not surprisingly, the doyen of South African journalists, Stanley Uys, wrote in August 1968 that if the *verligtes* took over power in South Africa, "the pattern of power politics will be much the same as it is now".[2] All the evidence thus suggests that the *verligte/verkrampte* debate in South Africa was in effect nothing but a public relations campaign : all words, no deeds, with the aim of buying time for apartheid.

It would be encouraging to report that such a gulf between promise and fact was the exception in South Africa. But the evidence says that it is not the exception, but the rule. The matter was put succinctly by the late Chief Albert Luthuli not long before his death. He said, "An honest examination of the facts always proves that it is impossible to defend South Africa's race policies without basing one's arguments on at least one basic and serious untruth."

There is strong evidence, then, that South African "publicity" material, or propaganda, does not reflect reality at all; that it is designed to misinform rather than to inform. But by what methods and techniques is this propaganda spread throughout the world, to such effect that even ordinary citizens in a variety of countries who are not quite sure how many of the Indian subcontinent's 650 million people are Indian, and how many Pakistani, have nevertheless heard in considerable detail of the alleged division of South Africa's two-and-a-half million Afrikaners into *verligtes* and *verkramptes*?

In fact, South African propaganda is disseminated throughout the world on several different levels, which reinforce each other by the principle of mutual support and consistency in repetition. The *modus operan*di can, in its essentials, be set out in general terms as follows (since many of the world's current misconceptions about South Africa have been the work of the now defunct South African Department of Information, and since that department's operations still continue world-wide through other South African government agencies, to avoid confusion the Information Department will be treated as if it still existed):

SOUTH AFRICAN EXTERNAL PROPAGANDA

1st Level: the government, its ministers and departments, especially the embassies and other overseas contacts.

1. Booklets, books and pamphlets, often sent unsolicited to important people.

2. Ministerial and other official speeches, interviews and talks, especially press conferences, within South Africa and overseas.

3. Regular locally-printed propaganda magazines issued in other countries by South African embassies (by 1975, these were being published in nine languages in twelve different countries, from Australia to Brazil).

4. Internal-propaganda magazines, mostly monthly; 24 in 13 different languages of southern Africa, with a heavy coverage

in the UN territory of Namibia illegally occupied by South Africa, in the Namibian languages.

5. Pre-recorded television films giving solely the government viewpoint on South Africa, shown in Western countries, plus arranged interviews with South African embassy officials to give the "truth" about South Africa.

6. Embassy-arranged seminars for businessmen and local cultural and political groups, to "explain" apartheid and encourage investment.

7. Books by government officials and pro-government academics, giving an "informed view" of South Africa.

8. Internal censorship of books, films, television programmes, radio, theatre and the banning and silencing without trial, and withholding of passports from the main critics of the government's policies, who could give the other side of the story, especially to the large number of foreign VIPs visiting South Africa.

9. The "buying" of foreign journalists. It was revealed by the department itself in a letter handed to a parliamentary committee in April 1978 that in order to lend credibility to the alleged independence of the Transkei, extra funds were requested for "the 'buying' of the services of a journalist who then ostensibly supplies 'independent' material for his publication while we pay him for his favourable opinion". The same official letter admitted that the alternative method of admitting only carefully selected journalists from overseas had drawbacks, as the Department of Information might "lose control over the eventual content", of the articles which resulted.[3]

2nd Level: Indirect sources, but government controlled.

1. South African Tourist Corporation and South African Airways—films, TV commercials, brochures, special trips for overseas VIPs ("soft" propaganda—only occasionally putting the government political and racial viewpoint strongly, but rarely if ever contradicting it).

2. Use of military, scientific, financial and even sporting officials visiting overseas countries to lobby influential people and spread basic propaganda.

3. The publicly-owned but government-controlled South African Broadcasting Corporation, which adheres strongly to official racial policy.

3—RPASA • •

3rd Level: Private South African sources, nearly all of them all-white, often heavily financed and keeping close to standard government propaganda themes. Plus overseas groups disseminating pro-apartheid propaganda, many of them now known to be secretly government-funded.

1. Groups and organizations of wealthy white South African businessmen often publishing expensive but almost wholly one-sided books and periodicals overseas, all openly or tacitly pro-government.

2. Groups claiming to represent all South African sportsmen, but white-controlled, and often spending large sums in defending the racial *status quo* in South African sport, through international lobbying, advertisements etc.

3. South African branches of international business associations (a typical example : one that flew in 231 guests from thirteen other countries for an "all expenses paid" tour of South Africa "to correct misrepresentations and give the true facts". All its guests were white, and only the white South African viewpoint was presented).

4. Trade organizations in other countries lobbying the interests of local industries with South African trade links. Some of these are overtly anti-black—one of them suggesting to a British parliamentary committee that black South Africans are mentally inferior to whites.

5. South African banks, industries, commercial groups and so on often produce their own South African "background" material, some of it quite expensive and much of it widely circulated throughout the world. Only the white viewpoint is usually given, although, as in much similar material, this is not always apparent and the arguments sometimes actually appear to be quite "objective".

6. Certain privately run groups in several Western countries, specializing in family visits between their own country and South Africa, at times indirectly receive financial aid from the South African government, and often hand out the government's pro-apartheid propaganda magazine to their members. All of them deny any political or racial bias. With rare exceptions, such groups are all-white, and may well be quite innocent.

7. Standard reference works on South Africa published in that country. Some of these simply omit facts and even whole subjects which might be considered to clash with the standard

white South African viewpoint. Others contain demonstrable government propaganda untruths. None give a balanced view of South Africa because some of the most important points they could mention of an anti-apartheid or anti-government nature cannot by law be published in South Africa—a fact which none of these reference works actually admits.

Miscellaneous : lobbying, public relations, censorship etc.

1. The aggressive tactics used by South African officials overseas in demanding local newspaper space and television time in order to "set the record straight" about apartheid need always to be set against a factor rarely mentioned—that passports are regularly refused to both black and white opponents of the South African government to travel overseas to give the other side of the story. (Example : a major policy speech by a South African cabinet minister in London late in 1975 was arranged only on the understanding that the other side of the case would be heard. After the minister had presented the pro-apartheid case, it was discovered that his government had refused a passport to the South African clergyman, Dr Beyers Naude, who had been booked to present the other side—which was thus never heard.)

2. "Blackmail" tactics—for many years, a carrot-and-stick technique has been used by the South African government to smooth the path—with import permits, etc.—for overseas firms operating in South Africa whose head offices defend South Africa; and to make things difficult or even impossible for other overseas firms whose head offices criticize apartheid in any way. (Example : the South African Radio Act as amended on 16 August 1966 allows the South African government to "name" foreign television and radio stations broadcasting anything to which the South African government objects. Overseas firms with South African branches—and indeed South African firms with overseas branches—taking advertising time on such foreign stations can be fined in multiples of £1,000 for such "crimes".)

3. Hidden censorship by group pressure. There are a variety of methods by which facts about South Africa can be—and indeed have been—censored overseas by commercial and other pressures. For instance, in July 1977 *The Guardian* reported a disturbing case, whereby many of South Africa's white-controlled libraries had threatened an economic boycott of all books

published in future by a well-known British publisher, unless
that publisher immediately abandoned plans to bring out an
already accepted book thought to be critical of white South
Africa and its government.

In fact the book tended to exonerate South Africa, but the
white librarians' threat of a mass boycott forced the British
publisher's South African agents to warn : "Our sales in South
Africa will be dramatically reduced if this book is published . . .
provincial libraries have already said that no further books of
yours should be submitted." The British publisher described
the South African librarians' action as an "unsubtle, brutish
form of censorship". (But in view of the fact that this kind of
censorship rarely gets reported, is it really that unsubtle? For
one of the most dangerous forms of censorship is that which
economic threats can buy, but which the press all too rarely
gets around to exposing. This South African boycott threat,
for instance—from a country fond of asserting that it never
supports boycotts—was reported, it seems, only by *The Guardian*.
And only in its gossip columns at that.)

An example of a more official attempt at censorship occurred
in 1978, when the South African government was advised that
the BBC was making a four -part television series on the
Afrikaner people. The government wrote to the Director-
General of the BBC urging that should South Africa find the
series unacceptable in any way, the BBC should broadcast a
corrective film on the subject made by the South African
government. Clear hints were made that unless the BBC did
as the South African government wished, both the position of
the BBC correspondents in South Africa and the lucrative purchase of BBC programmes by the government-controlled South
African Broadcasting Corporation would be the subject of a
"close new appraisal" by the South African government. The
BBC rightly rejected such threats.[4] But the series, in the view
of some, did seem tacitly pro-white.

4. Large numbers of influential foreign newsmen—editors,
journalists, commentators and so on—are invited to South
Africa on "see for yourself" luxury tours. Almost all are white,
and it has been estimated that more foreign editors visit South
Africa than any other country in the world. A subsidiary
exercise is the inviting of large numbers of scientists, industrialists, cultural leaders and so on of the West to South Africa

for specially arranged international seminars, at which the guests are lavishly entertained, often by skilled South African propagandists apparently unconnected with the government. The more influential of such guests find all their expenses paid for them. A recent practice is to encourage such visitors to buy property in South Africa—thus giving them an often unsuspected personal stake in preserving the racial *status quo* in South Africa—although they are never told that if they were black South Africans, they would be forbidden to buy such property.

5. Educational kits and books. A steady effort is maintained—with increasing success—to persuade educational publishers in the free world to publish special books or kits about South Africa—using information supplied only by the all-white South African government. By this means children outside South Africa are indoctrinated with tacit and often quite false racial or even anti-black propaganda, carrying the objective imprint of the innocent publisher.

6. "Scientific" seminars and symposia on the subject of race. It is not generally realized outside South Africa that what appear to be objective and even academically reputable organizations and theses devoted to the study of racial matters can be vehicles for the presentation of pro-apartheid propaganda. The South African Bureau of Racial Affairs, for instance, is a government-backed association which supports apartheid. Many Afrikaner professors in South Africa, sincere though they may be, are wholly committed to white supremacist doctrines (one such, a professor of zoology, once made the illuminating remark that he refused to teach the doctrine of evolution to his students because "it is not supported by Holy Scripture"). There are even allegedly disinterested scientific works on racial matters, to be found in many university libraries throughout the world and apparently quite unconnected with South Africa which, to quote the results of a thorough investigation into a major such work by a London *Sunday Times* research team in 1977, "resembled many other respectable academic texts but was South African inspired propaganda planned to bolster apartheid".[5] (In this particular case, the contributors appear to have been innocent; the work having been put together in a manner which apparently "supported" apartheid.)

7. Special South African "supplements". Large numbers of newspaper supplements have been published throughout the world about South Africa—nearly all strongly or tacitly favourable to the government and its racial policies—by the expedient of promising lucrative advertising support from the South African government, its agencies, and overseas companies with interests in South Africa. These supplements sometimes take the form of large, full-colour books—which the South African government subsidizes by pre-ordering quantities sometimes running into hundreds of thousands. These are then distributed free by South African embassies as "objective proof" of the "non-racist nature" of South African racial policies. Some apparently straightforward reportage books about South Africa in recent years have been indirectly subsidized by the South African government in this way.

8. Autobiographies, etc., by famous white South Africans. Sometimes achieving very heavy sales overseas, most such books whose authors still live in South Africa may well be honest and sincere, but often unconsciously give an insight into the world of racial misconceptions in which most white South Africans live, although their general effect is to reinforce the official racial propaganda themes which are spread by the government not only in the world at large, but within South Africa as well. Thus it is not unusual in such books to find passages such as this, in Mr Gary Player's *Grand Slam Golf* (Corgi Books, 1968) in a chapter entitled "My Country, 'tis of thee!" : "The African may well believe in witchcraft and primitive magic, practise ritual murder and polygamy; his wealth is in cattle. More money and he will have no sense of parental or individual responsibility, no understanding of reverence for life or the human soul which is the basis of Christian and other civilised societies." It is perhaps significant that, having earlier in the chapter referred to blacks in South Africa as "alien barbarians", this white South African in the very next paragraph repeated the untrue official version of South African history in which the blacks "moved down from Black Africa when the whites were establishing themselves" in South Africa. At the same time, it is not suggested that this book's author was doing anything but record typical white South African views on such matters.

9. Intimidation of critics overseas: Although it is true that some South African activities overseas against critics of apartheid

have been sensationalized and exaggerated, a hard core of cases remain—of intimidation, threats, bribes and smears. It is difficult to assess the effect of such activities, because often the evidence is negative—some South African exiles, for instance, threatened with action against relatives still in South Africa, do not inform the authorities in their new country and cease their anti-racist activities and writings in order to protect their relatives. The author of this book can, however, attest to the fact that smear campaigns are part of the South African armoury. After the publication of his first book on South African racial propaganda in 1968, he was the subject of extensive espionage by agents working for South African sources, culminating in the discovery on certain premises by a British journalist investigating other pro-South African espionage activities, of a sheet of paper in a known agent's handwriting, bearing this author's name and the words: "Frequently travels abroad. Purple hearts [drugs] and pornographic pictures to be placed in luggage and discovered in another country?"[6] Subsequent evidence linked such activities directly to a South African company controlled by several Afrikaner Nationalists not unconnected with the South African government. All such evidence was immediately placed in the hands of the appropriate authorities in Britain.

10. Discrediting activities: In 1978 an interesting case came to light. A black South African, now dead, who had been anti-government but dedicated to a policy of non-violence, and was also clearly non-Communist had for some years before his death been harassed and imprisoned by the South African police. In 1978 a book about him was published in Europe, allegedly by one of his best black friends. The book claimed that the dead dissident had really been committed to the violent overthrow of the South African government, and the creation of a Communist state in South Africa. But the dead man's own family and friends had never heard of the author of the book and its publisher could not be traced. Soon afterwards it was discovered that South African embassy officials in various countries were recommending the book to influential contacts as "the truth" about this and other black dissidents in South Africa, apparently in an attempt to discredit all such black dissidents.

11. Race Polarization Effect: Although five out of six South Africans are "non-white", almost all visitors to and from South

Africa are white, and all emigrants to South Africa must be white. A rough analogy would consist of only Arabs being able to leave Israel, and only Arabs being able to visit Israel; resulting in a built-in communication bias in the outside world's view of Israel, simply by biasing access to information, by religion and/or race.

12. Intimidation of blacks : various laws, including actual bannings, largely silence trenchant critics—especially black ones —of apartheid within South Africa. Black South Africans touring overseas are also "censored" : on 11 June 1971, in a policy statement, the Minister of the Interior said that passports are refused to non-white South Africans who "besmirch" their country or indulge in "more than normal" criticism of apartheid or the government. The South African press noted at the time that the South African Bureau of State Security routinely vets all non-whites applying for a passport.

CASE HISTORIES

The efficient and well-financed manner in which South Africa's mere 4.3 million whites spread their racial viewpoint even on the private level can be seen in two recent examples, one on a group level, the other aimed at private individuals throughout the world.

1   The American Legion. With a total of three million members, this right-wing organization of US war veterans possesses considerable lobbying power in American business and politics, its membership including two recent US presidents. The South African magazine *To The Point International* contained the news, in 1978, that the American Legion had launched a nation-wide campaign to "boost South Africa's image with the US government".

A five-member delegation from the American Legion had been lavishly entertained by influential white South Africans during a three-week visit to that country, at the invitation of a group of whites. As a result of the information they had been given during their visit, the Legion's National Convention agreed on actions including :

The lobbying of the US government to encourage investment in South Africa; to commit America more strongly to the purchase of South African raw materials; to re-introduce joint naval manoeuvres between the US navy and the South African navy; to treat minority-ruled South Africa at least as favourably as any black African state; and to recognize the Transkei "home-land" and thus endorse the South African racial policy.

The American Legion also resolved that its journal, the *Legionnaire,* would in future carry "a series of pro-South African articles", and that the Legion would "carry out extensive lobby-ing at grass roots and national level" and "promote mass media coverage of South Africa in the US". Although the report did not say so, all the activities with which the American Legion agreed to identify itself, happen to be identical to the views and interests of the minority Afrikaner Nationalist government of South Africa.

What did not appear to have been discussed, however, was the subversive anti-Allied and anti-American record of the Afrikaner Nationalist régime and of many of its current leaders in World War II. On the contrary, the report made clear that in this, as in so many other cases where white South Africa has lobbied overseas support, the key point was South Africa's alleged dedication to the cause of the West in combatting international communism. The fact that the South African navy has a whites-only command structure was also apparently not mentioned when joint US/South African naval exercises were being proposed.

2 "Operation Friendship." This was the name given to a nationwide South African public-relations exercise on the individual level, announced by Mr Vorster shortly before he became prime minister in 1966. It consisted of a state-aided plan encouraging white South Africans to write to friends and acquaintances abroad putting the white minority racial viewpoint.

In 1978, an interesting advertisement appeared in South Africa. It began by accusing British television of "brainwashing" the people of Britain about South Africa. (An odd accusation, as both black and white South African viewpoints are heard on British television, but only the white pro-apartheid view-point is normally heard on the government-controlled South African television services.) The advertisement went on to state that "as people overseas are given a less than totally balanced picture of the way things are in South Africa", South African readers were invited to hand over the names and addresses of relatives and friends abroad to the ten-year-old "friendship" organization named in the advertisement.

"More than 100,000 people abroad have already joined," claimed the advertisement, listing Britain, the USA, Canada, New Zealand and Australia as countries in which it already had well-established offices. It then promised free membership of its organization to all overseas people whose names were supplied to it—and further offered a variety of free inducements including ten free return air tickets to South Africa and 700 cash prizes ranging from R20 to R100, to those co-operating in its scheme.

Overseas members of the organization were also offered "news about South Africa", invitations to functions, film shows and "a host of other benefits". No indication was given as to who was financing the free membership and the ten free air tickets plus R25,000 worth of cash prizes.

But the information received by people outside South Africa whose names had been given to the organization had one thing in common. The news, views and "facts" were largely identical to the standard South African government propaganda themes spread throughout the world by South African embassies and fellow-traveller organizations.

The above is but a bare outline of some of the activities and methods by which the often falsely-based white South African view of apartheid is disseminated throughout the world, in places as various as German newspapers, British public schools, the American Congress and New Zealand business gatherings, while the viewpoint of the black South African majority even on the most urgent matters must usually depend on a few liberal newspapers, church groups, anti-racist organizations and an occasional book.

Yet even these few sources are the subject of attack by South Africa's white propaganda mouthpieces overseas—the most usual argument being to accuse those who try to present the viewpoint of the black South African majority of being "Communists" or "militant Leftists". Even so, the language used is frequently milder than that adopted by members of the South African government itself when describing much of the normal, informed criticism of apartheid by the parliaments and mass media of the Western world. One senior member of the government said in a speech in South Africa's all-white parliament in April 1975, for instance: "Our information officers abroad fight in the front line for South Africa against fanatical militant groups, hotbeds of leftist liberalism and Red onslaughts. They stand alone against forces of subversion and political terrorism; against double standards and against the lie. They stand like a David of old against the Goliath in their fight for South Africa."

On 4 March 1977, a cabinet minister in the South African parliament spoke of the activities overseas of the Department of Information. He said of apartheid's critics that "their words are now being thrown back at them and their hypocrisy unmasked. Vigorous action against smear campaigns, particularly those waged on British television, have made our opponents more wary. The success achieved by these aggressive methods has elicited a reaction among our traditional enemies. This proves that we have achieved success and that our actions have struck home. These people have been hurt."

The above passages tend to tell their own story of whether South African publicity activities overseas are merely normal "information" procedures, or whether South Africa is actively using its large and heavily financed propaganda organizations as an actual weapon, of psychological infiltration and bias.

Yet, as shown above, the official propaganda activities are only a small part of the overall story. And even this is not all. For it has been remarked that South Africa is itself a part of the propaganda operation—that is, even the daily life of the country tends to be deceptive because the white minority, after years of outside criticism of the racial policies they have created and so determinedly preserve, have become so unconsciously propaganda-minded that they tend even unwittingly to camouflage the reality when *uitlanders* (foreign businessmen or tourists) are around.

This could certainly explain the often glossed-over fact that many (white) people who go to South Africa for a visit, return defending that country—and not in their own words, but in exactly the same words and phrases, and often using the same discredited or racially biased arguments as their South African hosts and even the government Information Department's publications.

It is extremely difficult to refute most of these arguments if one has not also been to South Africa, or preferably lived there for a period of years. But as far as the racial content of such repeated propaganda is concerned, there is a simple enough technique which very often strips the argument down to its racially prejudiced essentials, and that is simply to transpose white and black in the statements made. Not only does this instantly illuminate the true nature of many governmental pronouncements (such as one which would then require a certain cabinet minister to refer to male *white* South Africans as "labour units" and their wives and children as "superfluous appendages") but it does severe damage to many of the rationales for the "black homelands" policy. For instance, simple transposition of government justifications of this policy then suggests that it is the *whites* who should thus be sent back to *their* homelands—of Holland, Britain and Germany—under a transposed "homelands" policy, and that it is the whites, not the blacks, who should be stripped of their South African citizenship and forced to negotiate Labour Contracts with the blacks before being allowed to work in South Africa. Similarly, any black would be allowed to move around South Africa to work and live as he pleased—but whites moving too far from their place of birth would (as blacks are now) be classed as "migrant labour" with no rights to negotiate their wages or even bring their families with them. The transposition technique is a valuable one, for it instantly identifies both racial propaganda, and the true nature of the racial attitudes and actions which the propaganda attempts to conceal.

It is also a technique which, with other methods of propaganda detection, should be used often, because it must be stated that those who have spent considerable time in examining the propaganda content of information, statements and even some "news" items originating with white South Africa, have come to the conclusion that a surprisingly high percentage of such data is overt or covert propaganda of some kind, even though it may appear to be quite innocent in nature. Therefore, in the interests of those at whom that propaganda is directed, it must also be noted that experience suggests it is unwise to believe any information from South Africa which even indirectly tends to support the racial *status quo* in that part of the world, until the main claims have been carefully checked. This may seem a Herculean task, but even if performed for only a short period it will be found that certain propaganda patterns soon emerge and one quite early learns to sift distortions from fact.

Taking all the evidence of South Africa's world-wide propaganda activities into account, it seems clear that the total sum spent on propaganda for apartheid by white South Africa must be many times greater than the R16 million per annum (about £9 million) probably still spent directly by the government. What, then, is the true source of such enormous sums of money? Ultimately, it is an unexpected one.

The British Broadcasting Corporation's *News at One* on Radio 4 on 26 December 1977, carried a special report on South Africa's luxurious Johannesburg-Cape Town "Blue Train". Spaciously accommodating little more than 100 passengers, all in private suites, and with superb service and five-course menus, the report noted that the Blue Train was heavily subsidized by South African Railways in order to make it the best train in the world—and thus a highly efficient public relations exercise for white South Africa.

Six months earlier, in June 1977 a black South African, Joyce Sikakane published a book *Window on Soweto*, in Britain. Detailing the daily life of that black township's one-and-a-quarter million inhabitants, the book noted that the government-owned South African Railways have admitted that their black commuter trains into Johannesburg from Soweto are so overcrowded that the sagging of the steel carriages causes the battery boxes underneath to hit the sleepers; and it further quoted a South African Railways' official statement that it makes more profit out of this black commuter line than out of any other part of the South African rail network.

In truth, then, the Blue Train which gives overseas visitors such a favourable impression of the *status quo* in South Africa is subsidized by overcharging the very section of the community which can least afford it, because it suffers most from the *status quo* of apartheid. The public relations exercise which helps divert attention from the inequalities of apartheid is thus paid for by the victims of apartheid.

This one example describes the whole. Official government propaganda and privately financed public-relations campaigns alike, all aimed at camouflaging the realities of apartheid and influencing overseas opinion in favour of continued white rule in South Africa, are at source really paid for by the cheap labour of the very group whose racial exploitation is thus disguised and concealed; an explanation of why there are so many hundreds of white millionaires in South Africa, and why so many whites can give such large sums to organizations committed to spreading propaganda for apartheid throughout the world.

This chapter began with a quotation from Adolf Hitler's *Mein Kampf*, which concluded : "The task of propaganda is to unite, and the task of the united is propaganda." Perhaps it should end by quoting a brief news item from *The Guardian*, London, of 25 November 1973 : "Africans living alongside main roads in South Africa should be given better quality housing so as to improve the country's image with foreign tourists, the government was told last week. Delegates to a tourism conference, held in Johannesburg by the Afrikaner Chamber of Commerce, called for the removal of roadside shanty homes. But they did not discuss African housing in general."

(In the Bibliography at the end of this volume will be found a list not only of those books which refute South Africa's official case for its racial policies, but also a list of a wide selection of South African government pro-apartheid books, booklets and magazines, and the addresses of the main South African embassies throughout the world from which they and similar literature can be obtained.

Perhaps it is worth repeating that no South African government information or "publicity" publication ever similarly includes a contra-list of *anti-apartheid* books and magazines, or gives any address from which such publications can be obtained. A fact which speaks for itself about that government's own view of the ability of its information material to stand up to informed scrutiny.)

PART TWO

THE PROPAGANDA THEMES

These are the more important of the carefully constructed propaganda arguments for South Africa's racial, economic and international policies. They are common coin within South Africa, at least amongst most whites, owing largely to the government's general control of the sole nationwide mass media—radio and television—and of school text books, education in government schools and censorship in the theatre and cinema.

Outside South Africa, more than £50 million in open, direct expenditure has been spent in the past ten years alone on the official dissemination of these themes. The amount spent on their international dissemination by undercover government means and by private organizations is incalculable.

However, comparison over a period of nearly fifteen years between the way these propaganda themes are presented abroad by the government, and by private South African sources, reveals little real difference. These, then, are the main propaganda distortions, which are still being officially spread worldwide, and which additionally would have been presented to the world under the guise of "the objective truth" about South Africa, if the extensive plans to bribe, control and subvert large sections of the free world's press had come unhindered to fruition in the 1970s.

CHAPTER THREE

The Basic Historical Deception

TO MAKE THE suggestion that much of the West's reporting
of, and public comment on the South African policy of apartheid
takes place on an almost entirely superficial level is to invite
strong reaction. After all, so many Westerners have been to
South Africa, reported on apartheid at great length and even
written books about it, that there does not appear to be much
more to be said. But, in reality, there is. For the entire policy,
and its central theme of dividing up South Africa into black
"homelands" on one hand, and "white South Africa" on the
other, is based on a deliberately fictionalized version of South
African history. The fact that the West now largely accepts
that counterfeit history, to such an extent that politicians and
press alike now use South African propaganda terms such as
"black homelands", "white South Africa", "black migrant
labour" and so on, represents one of the most remarkable,
worldwide propaganda successes in recent world history.

Yet South Africa's "selling" of a mostly fictitious version of
its racial history to the outside world in order to create some
kind of moral justification for its racial policies, is but part of
the story. Because the historical forgeries are themselves generally
unsuspected, so are the effects they are likely to have on South
Africa's early future. For here is a whole area of black discontent and a huge sense of injustice of the very kind which has
started most of mankind's bloodiest revolutions, and the West's
leaders and mass media are in effect completely unaware of it.

The nature and proofs of South Africa's enormous historical
deception could be set out at great length and in considerable
detail, contrasting again and again the official South African
claims and statements, and directly confuting them from the
researches and writings even of South Africa's own leading
historians and archaeologists. But in fact this is an area in which
science itself becomes directly involved, for the ultimate proofs
of South African deception come from something as non-

political and disinterested as radio-carbon atoms and their precise, immutable rate of decay. Carbon-dating techniques for the periods involved are today a very exact tool of the historian, and many of the sources given here and in the Bibliography show the extensive correlations between these and the many other dating methods used by archaeologists in South Africa.

This field of study is so well documented that the broad range of professional evidence entirely disproving South Africa's official justifications for apartheid and the "homelands" policy can be left to the books, journals and papers mentioned here. In this book, only the basic outline of the historical facts will be given. But in the case of the false version of South African history which has for years been presented to the world as the innocent *raison d'être* of apartheid, a little more detail is required. For this is the basic deception.

Essentially, the period of contention covers from about 1,000 years ago to less than 150 years ago. As will be seen, the key date is AD 1652, when the first white settlers arrived at the Cape of Good Hope, and founded Cape Town. These first whites to settle anywhere in what is now South Africa in fact clearly recorded at the time that they stole the land from its original inhabitants, and it must be mentioned that there are one or two oblique references to this in South African propaganda.

Generally, however—quoting the official government literature and statements by politicians and diplomats—the authorized version of South Africa's racial history which has for years been spread throughout the world by every possible means, goes like this :

The South African government's version of history
While it is true that the first white settlement anywhere in South Africa was that at Table Bay on the site of Cape Town in AD 1652, under Jan van Riebeeck, the government claims that up until that time there had been no blacks (Bantu) at all anywhere in South Africa, the very first blacks arriving at about the same time, or later, than the whites. Thus : "The Bantu crossed the northern frontiers of what is today the Republic of South Africa at about the same time as the white settlers started opening up the country from Table Bay" states *South African Quiz*, published by the South African embassy

in London in 1968. Amongst many basically identical statements one could quote an earlier one: "The Bantu crossed
what are today the northern borders of South Africa at about
the same period in history when the Dutch landed at the Cape"
(*South Africa Today*, No. 27, published in 1964 by the South
African Department of Information); a much later one:
"Towards the middle of the 17th century the white and black
peoples of southern Africa converged in what was then an
almost uninhabited part of the continent" (the South African
Representative to the UN, to the United Nations Security
Council on 24 October 1974); and: "the Bantu are the descendants of the black immigrants who invaded South Africa from
the north at about the same time as the first Europeans settled
at the Cape" (i.e., in the mid-seventeenth century), says the
State of South Africa Year Book for 1977, page 23. Indeed,
according to the South African Ambassador in Britain in an
official article in the magazine *The Diplomatist* for December
1964, when the first whites arrived at the Cape in AD 1652,
South Africa consisted of "totally uninhabited territories". And
a related source, a one-time Director of Information in the same
embassy, claimed in 1977 in his book *The World, the West and
Pretoria* (David McKay Inc. USA) that when the first whites
settled in South Africa the nearest Bantu were more than 1,200
miles away; no closer than Lourenço Marques in Mozambique.

The next important date in this official version of South
African history is AD 1770. The first black/white contact was
"not until 1770", say sources such as *Multi-National Development in South Africa*—published by the government in 1974 in
Pretoria. This first contact was allegedly at the Great Fish River,
on the coast in the southern-eastern corner of South Africa, 500
miles from Cape Town. Decades of intermittent warfare followed between Boer and Bantu.

In the 1830s the Great Trek began, of Boers anxious to escape
from the more liberal British influence then being felt at the
Cape. The official version begins to contradict itself here. In
the previous two or three decades an internal conflict between
black groups, the *mfecane*, had heavily reduced the number of
blacks in the Transvaal particularly, although many thousands
still lived there. Some official sources (such as the government-
controlled South African Broadcasting Corporation on 16 August

1965) have insisted that the land the trekkers entered—the Orange Free State, Transvaal and Natal—was "empty and uninhabited". Other sources (*South Africa Today*, April 1964, Department of Information) equally emphatically assert that in the Transvaal the Boer trekkers repeatedly met "marauding hordes of Bantu". By 1974 the South African Ambassador to the UN was telling that body that all three provinces entered by the Boers were "for the most part completely uninhabited", despite the fact that the journals of the trekkers themselves record repeated clashes with the black inhabitants of these "uninhabited" lands.

At this point the official version of history becomes quite unspecific as to actual areas and dates. "The areas originally settled remained the traditional homelands of different groups. This was neither colonialism nor conquest," says *Progress Through Separate Development*, published by the Information Service of South Africa in New York in 1973. Later the same book claims that "the Bantu . . . fled to him [the white man] for protection, driven out of their own homelands by internecine strife and tyranny". But how this came about, and who the alleged tyrants were, is not mentioned, although under the significant heading "Historical encounter in Vacant Land", the same source insists that neither the white nor black settlers annexed the other's territory "or robbed him by invasion and oppression".

On this period between 1840 and the early years of this century, the official version is largely silent, picking up the threads again at 1910 or later, by which time it is claimed that "history itself" had demarcated South Africa as one-eighth black and seven-eighths white, "without the necessity of white or black intruding an inch on the areas which each group had already settled". Or as Mr Vorster himself put it in parliament in 1966, shortly after becoming prime minister : "The fact that 13 per cent of the land in the Republic is Bantu and 87 per cent is occupied by whites is a division decreed by history."[1]

Finally, some South African sources now suggest that South Africa's cities and white farms are on land that no black man trod until long after the cities had been built and most of the farms established. "For half a century blacks have left their tribal homelands to work in the white areas," said the commentary of the South African government film *Black Man*

Alive shown on BBC-2 television in Britain on 12 December 1974, implying that before that, all blacks stayed in their "homelands".

The official version in brief is, then, that white and black reached South Africa at the same time, little more than three centuries ago, prior to which South Africa was largely or totally uninhabited; that black and white first met 500 miles east of Cape Town in 1770 as both groups were expanding; that they somehow settled quite different areas without conflict and without the whites taking any land that was originally black; that 87 per cent of South Africa is therefore historically white because the whites were the first to settle it; and that the whites now generously allow the blacks to leave their homelands and work in the more prosperous areas—"white" South Africa. This is the moral justification of both the "black homelands" policy and of apartheid itself, which now claims that as the black majority never lived in any of the 87 per cent of South Africa which is "white homeland", then the blacks have no right even to South African citizenship, which is therefore now being taken away from them.

There is, however, an interesting omission in all such official material describing South Africa's history. Few proper historical authorities are ever quoted, despite the fact that both South African and overseas historians and archaeologists have for decades been unravelling, with spade, radio-carbon datings and pre-1652 Portuguese naval documents, the undeniable facts about the major pre-white racial events in South Africa over the past 1,000 years and more. And perhaps the reason for such a lack of documentation lies in the fact that the professional historians' version of South African history does not so much confirm the official apartheid version, as reveal it as untenable fiction, almost in its entirety.

The scientifically documented version of South Africa's history was even emerging twenty years before the present political version had been put together, so some of the most important facts which discredit the propaganda version were known before it was created. The carefully documented professional historians' version of South Africa's racial history follows. There is much more to it than the events described below, but the salient claims and dates of the whites' racial and political version may now usefully be compared with the proper historical record.

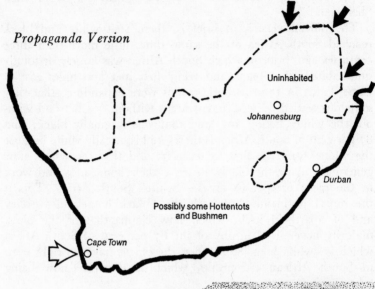

Propaganda Version

Uninhabited

○ Johannesburg

○ Durban

Possibly some Hottentots and Bushmen

Cape Town ○

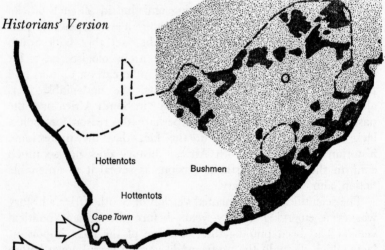

Historians' Version

Hottentots

Bushmen

Hottentots

Cape Town ○

⇨ First white settlers arrive (historically correct).

◆ First Bantu allegedly beginning to enter South Africa.

▓ True overall extent of Bantu settlement when whites first arrived (apartheid's so-called "Bantu homelands" shown in black, for comparison). Also see frontispiece.

The historical facts

Although the maps and statements of the all-white South African government quite clearly claim that the blacks, or Bantu as they will be specifically called now, did not enter South Africa until the seventeenth century AD, they were in fact already settled in parts of South Africa by the tenth century AD, and quite possibly even earlier.

Settlement by Africans of one kind or another over a good deal of what is now South Africa has been proved as far back as 20,000 years ago,[2] but their exact description is uncertain. By very roughly 2,000 years ago, Africans of the Early Iron Age were settling extensively in South Africa, or were perhaps already there and were undergoing cultural changes as the first iron-smelting technologies filtered down from the north. There are clear cultural—and thus inevitably biological—links between these Early Iron Age peoples and those of the Later Iron Age, or Bantu, peoples whose increasingly widespread settlement of South Africa dates from at least 1,000 years ago. Thus the ancestors of most of the present-day Bantu inhabitants of South Africa—today's 19½ million black South Africans—were already in South Africa 1,000 years ago, and some of these ancestors were there 2,000 or more years ago.[3]

Although the South African goverment has, interestingly enough, shown considerable reluctance in supporting archaeological work, a wide spectrum of both South African and overseas archaeologists has for many years been assembling the country's pre-white history, and some of the well-established professional findings can be touched on here to show just how far from the truth is the official version of history by which apartheid is allegedly justified.

Proof that there were Bantu in South Africa 1,000 years ago has, amongst other evidence, been clearly established by Scully and van der Merwe, writing in *World Archaeology* in October 1971. Their extensive research, backed by consistent radiocarbon datings, shows that the BaPhalaborwa tribe now living around the rich copper and phosphate deposits at Phalaborwa in the northern Transvaal had been living there continuously since at least AD 960, had been experienced miners with sophisticated smelting techniques, and had enjoyed a good and varied diet. (Today, the rich mineral deposits are classed by the government as part of the "traditional white South African homeland", despite the existence of many ancient Bantu mining tunnels up to 50 feet deep.)

Scattered across the Transvaal and Orange Free State "white homelands" of South Africa are hundreds of stone-walled, Bantu-built settlement sites, many of them dated to more than 900 years ago. One of them, a smelting furnace radio-carbon dated to AD 1060, is actually inside a "whites-only" Johannesburg inner suburb, Melville Koppies, and is almost on top of the Main Gold Reef, which white South Africa claims belongs to whites because of "prior white settlement". The frontispiece shows 11th-16th century Bantu sites on the southern edge of Johannesburg, on "whites-only" farmland less than five miles from the notorious apartheid black township of Soweto, whose inhabitants may not own land anywhere near Johannesburg because it was allegedly "first settled by whites, not blacks".

Many of the Bantu stone-built sites across the northern half of South Africa are of similar date—mainly from the thirteenth to fifteenth centuries AD—and known to have been built by the Sotho and Venda peoples who have ever since then formed a substantial part of the South African population.[4] At an approximately similar period, much of the south-east of South Africa, from Mozambique to the Great Fish River, was settled by the *nguni* (Bantu) peoples. The whites did not arrive in South Africa at all until the seventeenth century, and did not reach this area until the eighteenth century—by which time the *nguni*—Xhosa, to be exact—had already reached Mossel Bay, only 200 miles from Cape Town.[5] Today's white propagandists ignore this fact, even though it is attested to by their own ancestors, from whose explorers' diaries this fact is taken. It is pretended today that this historic first white/Bantu contact took place 70 years later, 500 miles from Cape Town.

Here, too, the "whites and blacks arrived at about the same time" story receives another death-blow. In June 1552—exactly 100 years before the first white settlement—the Portuguese vessel *San Joao* was wrecked on the Pondoland coast, 150 miles south of where Durban now stands. The survivors' diaries record that they met "very black" Africans who spoke in a clicking tongue: a description which fits only Bantu. Yet as recently as April 1977 the South African Education Department's magazine *Bantu* was still putting forward the long-discredited official version of history, as the basis of history teaching in black schools and colleges in South Africa.

South Africa's white children are similarly indoctrinated. Between the beginning of the nineteenth century and the Great Trek of Boers in the 1830s, as noted earlier, the black civil war, the *mfecane* had greatly reduced the black populations of the Transvaal and Orange Free State areas, but had certainly not eliminated them, a fact attested to by post-*mfecane* but pre-Trek explorers such as Robert Moffat. But the Afrikaner Nationalist magazine *Patrys*, for instance, distributed in Afrikaner schools throughout South Africa, in its May 1976 issue in a pictorial "history lesson" shows that young Afrikaners are taught that at the time of the Great Trek, the only Bantu in South Africa were the Xhosas in the Transkei and the Zulus in Zululand. With the exception of these and a few Vendas in the far west, all South Africa is shown as still uninhabited by Bantu.

The reality, according to the professional historians, is that by then roughly half of South Africa had long been settled by Bantu. (And so it is fair to suggest that these areas, half the country, by the South African government's own definition are the true "black homelands".) Yet when the whites arrived, the rest of South Africa was by no means empty. Roughly south of centre were the Bushmen, and the southernmost portion in the west had been settled by Hottentots for many centuries beforehand. Far from being "totally uninhabited", South Africa was fully inhabited, with perhaps a million brown and black people already there. In contrast, an official assessment as late as AD 1810 showed that even then, there were barely 30,000 whites in the whole of South Africa.[6]

Three facts are thus fully established. The whites were by far the late-comers in South Africa. Whether one's point of reference is the time of the first white settlement in AD 1652 or the time of the major black/white contacts a century later, the blacks occupied a good one-half of South Africa before the whites arrived. And blacks have always greatly outnumbered whites in South Africa—so it is thus by definition a black man's country rather than a white man's, despite white propaganda claiming exactly the opposite.

After the Great Trek of the Boers in the 1830s, written history and official contemporary documents take up the story : of the wars, skirmishes and massacres, the agreements, the treachery on both sides and the whites' ultimate armed conquest of every last corner of South Africa, although many of these facts are today denied in modern government publicity material—and even in the United Nations, where on 23 October 1974 South Africa's white representative claimed in a major speech: "We have stolen land from nobody. We have conquered no people."

But such professional archaeologists as Prof. Brian Fagan, writing in *Southern Africa in the Iron Age* (Thames & Hudson 1965) which traces the history of the Iron Age—i.e., Bantu—people of southern Africa, state: "The story of the nineteenth century in South Africa is one of continuous clashes between the interests of Boer and British and those of the Iron Age peoples who had been settled in the eastern, central and northern parts of the South African interior for many centuries." (Page 166).

The end result of those clashes was the establishment of the Native Reserves, mostly in remote and poverty-stricken rural areas, and representing only shrunken remnants of some of the whole "eastern, central and northern" part of South Africa which had been settled by blacks long before the first whites arrived. The Reserves eventually became Bantustans, and these in turn became the "black homelands"—allegedly all that the black man had ever settled—"a division decreed by history," as Mr Vorster has put it.

13.7 per cent of the whole was all of South Africa that was ever settled by the blacks, according to today's white politicians; but at least half of the whole had been settled by blacks for centuries, according to the professional historians. The latter have science and contemporary eye-witness reports behind them. The former must by the very nature of their claims deny the existence of millions of tons of pre-white Bantu stone ruins, scattered across hundreds of square miles of "white" South Africa (indeed, the government-controlled South African Tourist Corporation has denied that the Bantu built in stone at all). A very small section of these ruins, on the very edge of Johannesburg, is shown in the frontispiece, and can be seen by any visitor who hires a plane from nearby Baragwanath aerodrome, less than five miles away.

Is the South African government perhaps innocently unaware of the true history of the country it governs? All the evidence suggests that it is not. The first few pages of the popular book

Barrier of Spears (Timmins, Cape Town, 1973), a history of the Drakensberg mountains of Natal by R. O. Pearse, one of South Africa's most respected educationists and historians, carry the statement that when van Riebeeck, the leader of the first white settlers, "arrived at the Cape in AD 1652, most of South Africa was already occupied by Bantu-speaking peoples". *Barrier of Spears* has an enthusiastic Foreword by a South African cabinet minister. Other books published in South Africa and which contain the professionally-gathered historical facts, available for all to read, include *Archaeology in Southern Africa* (Woodhouse, Purnell, Cape Town, 1971), and an entire compendium of pre-white black settlement: *Bibliography of South African Pre- and Proto-Historic Archaeology,* published by the government's own Department of Education, Arts and Science in Pretoria in 1966.

Perhaps the final words can be left to the South African historian Dr Freda Troup, who in *South Africa—an Historical Introduction* (Eyre Methuen 1972) wrote: "When the Dutch were making their first settlement in the extreme south-west the Bantu-speaking people had already been living in the northern, central and eastern parts for as much as several hundred years." And to the world-recognized African historian Basil Davidson, writing in *Europa Year Book—Africa South of the Sahara: 1977–78.* Mr Davidson summed up this aspect of South African history by noting that when the "first Dutch settlers began encroaching on their lands", the Bantu had already "been in South Africa for the best part of a thousand years".

The South African government's deliberately rewritten version of its country's history has, in fact, been described by a British historian as of the same order of falsity as a British government persistently claiming, for self-interested political reasons, that when William the Conqueror's fleet arrived off the south coast of England in AD 1066, it was repulsed by Sir Francis Drake and the English fleet, assisted by Admiral Nelson in the *Victory*.

How the Bantustan policy shares the land
The very size of the disparity in land share compared with racial population under the "black homelands" policy shows clearly enough that whites get far more land than blacks in South Africa—although South African "information" literature never directly admits this. Where it even indirectly admits it,

it focuses attention instead on other matters such as relative annual rainfall, while comparison of land areas of the "homelands" is made not with the area of "white" South Africa, but with Wales or Switzerland, 6,000 miles away (a very common South African red herring).

Perhaps the reason for such odd comparisons can be seen in a little arithmetic so simple that one would expect its interesting results to be common knowledge throughout the West. But as far as can be discovered, the West's journalists, commentators and "authorities" on South Africa have never even attempted it. Yet the data are well known, and not in doubt.

South Africa has a total area of 472,000 square miles. Of this only 13.7 per cent or 65,000 square miles are the white-ordained black "homelands" or Bantustans, while 86 per cent or 406,000 square miles (leaving a few hundred square miles for the almost landless Asian and Coloured three million) is the "traditional white homeland", or "white South Africa".

There are (1978 figures) 4.3 million white South Africans, and 19 million black South Africans. Since the blacks may only vote, enjoy human rights, run businesses and own property in the 65,000 square miles of their "homelands", it is easy enough to work out that the white-created "homelands" policy means that more than 290 blacks must share each square mile of the black "homelands", while only $10\frac{1}{2}$ whites share each square mile of "white" South Africa.

That is to say, the Bantustan Policy, created by the white South African minority as the "fair and just solution" of the racial problem in South Africa, actually gives each white, on average, 28 times more land—and its underlying mineral wealth —than each black.

This figure of a 28-to-1 land discrimination against black South Africans is significant enough by itself. But if one applies this same discriminatory ratio against white South Africans instead of black ones, the true nature of this racial disproportion in land shares is more easily grasped, and its alleged "fairness" can be instantly assessed.

Thus, if—for example—South Africa had an all-black government which had an identical "homelands" policy under which *blacks, per capita*, got 28 times more land than *whites*, then all South Africa's 4.3 million white people would have less than one per cent of South Africa—less than 4,000 square miles

—to call their own. (In this case, population densities would, in round figures, be 40 blacks per square mile and 1,150 whites per square mile.)

In human terms, it would seem that this is what the "home-lands" policy is really all about: a racial disproportion of land so great, that the actual figure is never mentioned. Yet that figure attains even greater importance when it is set against South Africa's attempts to gain international recognition for its "autonomous" black homelands of Bophuthatswana, the Transkei and so on.

The countless millions of pounds spent by South Africa in lobbying and propaganda expenses during its campaigns to get its allegedly independent black homelands recognized, make sound economic sense if one simply considers one fact. And that is that international recognition for even one "independent" homeland such as the Transkei will set a precedent for eventual international recognition of them all, which will give an irrever-sible international seal of approval to a racial division of land in South Africa under which a white is, on average, entitled to a 28 times bigger share than a black. The anti-black policy of apartheid, with its small black homelands based on a counterfeit version of history, will have been accepted as respectable by the international community. This is the real reason for South Africa's determination to get the West to recognize at least one black homeland.

That South Africa has indeed put a huge and long-term effort into its attempt to "sell" the alleged homelands policy to the world can be seen indirectly by an interesting piece of evidence. As should by now be clear, the official version of South African history is characterized by a series of plausibly devised untruths. But they are untruths essential to any attempt to "sell" the Bantustan policy overseas. Therefore, where one finds influential people or organizations overseas repeating with some exactitude the largely untrue official version of South Africa's racial history, then one has probably pin-pointed an area where a strong attempt has been made by white South Africa to get acceptance for the Bantustan policy and its hidden racism of 28 times more land for a white than for a black. For unless some such theory is true, there is no possible reason why South Africa should have put great effort into propounding a version of its history known to be false, and thus liable at some time in the future to discredit its creators. There is further evidence of this.

In the case of any particular event or situation, there is only one true way to describe that event, but a practically unlimited number of untrue ways to describe it. It is one of the truisms of the technique of detecting propaganda falsehoods, that where one finds just one out of a large number of possible falsehoods being repeated by a variety of different sources, then this is proof enough that a determined effort has been made to get this particular falsehood accepted as the truth, by those whom the falsehood will benefit in some way.

The evidence that the palpably untrue version of South Africa's history specifically favoured by the South African government has indeed been spread throughout the world, and is now in many influential quarters accepted as the truth, is not hard to find. The innocent believers of such propaganda are from all walks of life. As long ago as 1963, the October issue of the South African edition of the *Reader's Digest* carried part of the all-white government's version of history in an article pleading for "more time" for South Africa, written by a US presidential adviser.

In more recent years, there is the interesting statement in the superbly-produced 330-page coffee-table book *What About South Africa* (International Auge, Mexico, 1971) that when the first white settlers landed at Table Bay in 1652 AD, apart from "a few nomadic Hottentots . . . this fabulous country lay undisturbed by human inhabitants". The South African government bought 150,000 copies of this publication and mailed it free to influential politicians, industrialists, journalists and opinion-formers throughout the world.

In 1969, Britain's Standard Bank Group, which has extensive South African interests, was, in an expensive free booklet, "South Africa, Land of Sunshine and Opportunity", telling potential (white) British emigrants to South Africa—many of them its own customers and shareholders—that "The Bantu came from the north at about the same time as the first Europeans settled at the Cape".

Two years later the British bank, Barclays DCO of London, was telling its British customers and shareholders in its glossy, full-coloured booklet, "Emigrating to South Africa", that "The Bantu moved south into what is now South Africa, arriving there at about the same time as the first whites were establishing themselves at the Cape".

In its June 1973 issue *Armed Forces Journal International,* an influential American magazine circulated to armed-forces chiefs throughout the free world and extensively circulated within the Pentagon, carried a special fifteen-page supplement on South Africa. The introductory article, "A Policy of 'Separate Development' ", quoted white South Africans as saying "Our ancestors arrived in this country (South Africa) to find vast, undeveloped areas that were virtually unpopulated. . . . The Bantu came later, attracted partly by the prosperity and security created by white vigour and industry".

Of this claim that the whites actually arrived in South Africa before the Bantu, the magazine commented in parenthesis : "The South Africans are historically correct here. Settlers in South Africa found only a few stone-age bushmen and Hottentots . . . the Bantus began arriving in what is now South Africa about the same time or a little later for the most part." The magazine gratefully acknowledged the source of this information as "the South African embassy in Washington".

In the early 1970s two special education kits for schools were produced about South Africa, one in America and the other in Britain. Both extensively utilize material supplied by the South African government and both put forward the false government version of South African history, in which whites and blacks arrived "at about the same time".[7]

On 12 December 1974, as remarked on earlier, the British Broadcasting Corporation's BBC-2 TV programme broadcast, in the interests of "balance" an official South African government film, *Black Man Alive.* This included the government's version of South Africa's racial history, with an animated map which showed black and whites arriving at about the same time, with the blacks avoiding the Transvaal areas where their pre-white ruins have for years been known to abound. As far as can be established, although the BBC has thus shown the untrue version of South Africa's history, it has never in any similar peak listening time shown the true version.

Visitors to South Africa are apparently unwittingly indoctrinated with the official version of history—sometimes in an extreme form—on the spot. In the book *The Other Side of the Coin—a Visit to South Africa* by Patience Strong (Backman &

Turner, London, 1976) is the interesting statement: "The Bantu ... were not indigenous. They came after the Dutch and the British." A similar version is found in Alan Drury's *A Very Strange Society* (1968). And many books published in South Africa for world-wide consumption carry much the same story. "Bantu tribes from Central and East Africa invaded South Africa at the time when Europeans landed at the Cape," asserts the privately-published *State of South Africa Year Book* (note that blacks "invade", but whites merely "land"), in issue after issue. Unsolicited free copies of this book have been received year after year by influential politicians and industrialists throughout the world. The source of such generosity is unknown.

The above examples are only a small fraction of the evidence available to show that a determined campaign has for many years been in progress on a global basis, in which great effort and vast sums have been spent in propagating the official, but long-discredited government version of South Africa's racial history, without which neither the "homelands" policy nor apartheid itself can even remotely be morally or historically justified. And so it is interesting to record that while this book was being written, the above assertion was given unexpected support by the South African Department of Information itself.

Amongst evidence of intended bribery of foreign journalists by that department, revealed in the course of a government enquiry and published by the South African and world press, was a letter written in 1976—the year of the Transkei "homeland's" so-called independence—to South Africa's Treasury by the head of the Department of Information. A section of this letter read: "A point that should not be missed is that if the independence of the Transkei is not convincingly promoted, the whole policy of the government will fall flat in the eyes of the world. It is the cornerstone on which the structure of future constitutional and political development is to be built. In the event that other governments in Africa, Europe and the Americas do not recognize the State of Transkei, hundreds of millions of rands will have been wasted."[8]

The "self-governing black homelands" today
The fact, established again and again over many years by South Africa's own professional historians and archaeologists, that the

"black homelands" or Bantustan policy is based largely on a
fictitious version of history, and that in mathematical terms the
policy gives each white man nearly 30 times more land than
each black man, puts an entirely altered perspective on the
"homelands" stratagem.

There is, to be true, a great deal of proof that even the new
"autonomous" states of Bophuthatswana and the Transkei are
neither autonomous nor free. There is proof that again and
again, when white South Africa perceives a valuable asset—
whether it be scenic or mineral—in a "self-governing black
homeland", it simply takes it for itself and redraws the bound-
aries if necessary (the case of now-white Phalaborwa and its
continuous 1,000 years of black settlement and mining is but
one example of many; the valuable Blyde River Canyon area
is another).[9] And there are proofs of South Africa's bad faith
in the matter of the black "homelands" which are simply a
matter of common sense, so great are the flaws in the official
explanations of the policy.

One example: if the Transkei, for instance, were truly as
South Africa claims a totally independent country in the same
way that "France and Germany are independent from England"
—to quote the government's publicity material—then a black
Transkeian would surely have the same rights, when visiting or
working in Johannesburg or Cape Town, as a white Canadian
or Englishman. But he does not. The moment the black Transkeian steps outside the Transkei, he comes under the full force
of South Africa's racial apartheid laws, and cannot enjoy even
the most basic rights which are on the other hand instantly
granted to the white English or Canadian visitor or immigrant.
And this even if the black Transkeian concerned has actually
been born in Johannesburg or Cape Town.

The point is particularly well illustrated in the case of the
thousands of "illegal black migrants" who in 1977 and 1978
had their homes bulldozed into rubble near Cape Town. Yet
they are as genuinely South African as the whites operating
the bulldozers.

In fact, all blacks are considered "foreigners" in the Western
Cape Province, as the whites claim that they had settled this
area before any Bantu arrived there. The claim is true—but
the obverse is never mentioned—that in that case, whites
should be classed as "foreigners" in Natal, the Orange Free

State and the Transvaal, because the blacks undoubtedly settled these areas before any whites arrived *there*.

But that is not all. While a white man from Finland or New Zealand may easily go to any part of South Africa to work and settle, no black man at all—even if he has actually been born there—may work and live as of right in the Western Cape Province; a practice now being extended to all of "white" South Africa. Thus, the reason given by the authorities for their demolition of thousands of blacks' homes near Cape Town was that their occupants had no right to be in South Africa, had no work permits, and mostly came from the "autonomous" Transkei anyway. The authorities denied that their action was in any way due to the colour of the victims' skins.

Yet *whites* born in the Transkei or even in Namibia have automatic South African citizenship and may go to Cape Town to work without a permit, and stay there all their lives without a single objection being raised. (Altogether, more than two million non-white South Africans have so far been uprooted from their homes and deported often hundreds of miles under the whites' so-called resettlement policies—an act of mass cruelty given minimal attention by the West's press and television. One cannot help speculating on the publicity that would have been forthcoming had it instead been a *black* minority government thus uprooting two million *whites* from their homes.)

There are so many such gaps in the "logic" of both apartheid and the homelands policy that the reader is best served by referring to the Bibliography, since there is a good literature on the subject. And in any case, as noted earlier, the overwhelming importance of the historical aspect of the homelands policy makes those aspects which have received almost all the attention by the world's governments, press and television largely irrelevant. If the title deeds to a property are found to have been forged, continual argument over the behaviour of those actually living on the property must ultimately be counted either as a waste of time—or perhaps as a diversionary tactic to draw attention from certain damning historical truths which seem to have been the victims of an extraordinary, world-wide conspiracy of silence.

And—to quote a recognized historian—if in South Africa even the known scientific facts of that country's racial history can be twisted out of all recognition for racial reasons, and this white supremacist fiction presented as "the truth" in years-long, multi-million pound propaganda campaigns throughout the world, then how much credence can be placed on anything that white South Africa says in defence of apartheid?

The question is not a rhetorical one. For on its answer hangs not only the viability of the West's policies towards southern Africa in general, but in some measure the West's overall attitudes on race and colour, as well; attitudes watched keenly by that three-quarters or more of the world's population whose skins are "non-white".

South Africa is watching, too—and apparently making cosmetic adjustments in the hope that world opinion can still be persuaded that if only the white minority responsible for apartheid can be given more and more time, all will be well. For in January 1979 Prime Minister P. W. Botha made a widely reported policy speech in which he put forward the idea that there was a possibility that more land might, eventually, be made available to black South Africans.

But even the pro-government press in South Africa noted that nearly two million acres of land promised to the blacks in 1936 had still not been given up by the whites, and the additional areas now vaguely pledged are in any case much too small to materially alter the huge racial imbalance in land shares, based on an untenable and largely discredited historical "justification" of apartheid.

CHAPTER FOUR

Job Reservation and the Income Gap

JOB RESERVATION

On 23 January 1978, Britain's Foreign Secretary announced that the new Codes of Employment Practice for British and European companies operating in South Africa had as their objective "to erode apartheid at its foundations". But only a few months earlier, a spokesman for the now banned and silenced Christian Institute of South Africa had publicly warned the West: "If the South African black people have to suffer, they want to suffer with hope and with an end in sight. Ameliorating measures, such as codes of employment practices, have provided no hope. They will never end apartheid."

The facts appear to be on the side of the Christian Institute, because not only—as will be seen—do the white-made laws of South Africa specifically prevent any code of employment practice from properly eroding apartheid in any way (merely allowing such codes to treat some of apartheid's more obvious symptoms), but the West appears to have been following a false trail. The name of this trail is a familiar one—Job Reservation—and Western governments and companies alike have apparently been led to believe that its abandonment will somehow abolish apartheid in employment. Indeed, some Western firms have been persuaded that Job Reservation somehow helps the blacks. "Job Reservation is applied not only to keep wages stable, but also to assist in creating separate non-white industries, businesses and trades in order to build up non-white areas as separate economically viable units," Barclays Bank was reassuring its British customers and shareholders in 1971.[1]

But in fact, Job Reservation is but a minor side-effect of the basic laws which entrench white domination in employment in South Africa. If Job Reservation were entirely abolished, those anti-black employment laws would remain relatively unharmed; a point which very few sections of the mass media understand.

The London *Times*, for instance, on 16 December 1977 head-lined a report "South Africa scraps half its job reservation laws", but the report itself showed no sign of any awareness of the existence of the overall anti-black employment decrees and legislation of which Job Reservation is but one specialized section affecting at most 2.9 per cent of the black South African work force, according to the South African government's own statement in the same week.

The British government, too, has shown reluctance to examine the causes of racism in South African employment, preferring to discuss the symptoms. The 1973 British parliamentary select committee which examined the employment practices of British firms in South Africa confined itself almost exclusively to the symptoms—low black wages and lack of union representation—instead of the disease, the racial laws themselves, which render any treatment a mere temporary palliative.

With about five billion pounds of British money currently invested in South Africa, it would seem reasonable to suggest that a full examination of racial employment practices there is a matter of some urgency and importance. Quite apart from the moral aspects, if the black work force is not, as white South Africa would have the West believe, relatively content but is instead so economically oppressed that it may even be fomenting a revolution, then the West needs to know about it. But instead, the West appears to believe South African propaganda sug-gesting that Job Reservation is the sole culprit.

Such propaganda, picked up by the mass media of the West, has been appearing for years all over the world. In addition, extensive publicity has lately been given to promises of pro-motion without regard to race in South Africa. These had begun during 1977 when the Cape Town Chamber of Com-merce—almost exclusively white—issued a manifesto pledging, to quote the (inevitably white) head of a large South African mining company, to "Select, employ, train and promote staff without regard to race or colour".[2] Later, the Deputy Head of the South African government's Department of Information himself echoed this to a special seminar of British businessmen at South Africa House in London on 6 May 1977 : "Members of the Cape Town Chamber of Commerce have pledged them-selves in writing to select, employ, train and promote staff regardless of race". The same source at the same time quoted

an unnamed London stockbroker as stating that in South
Africa, "Job Reservation in industry has nearly disappeared".[3]

This and much other material, some official, some privately
published, has without doubt given the clear impression that
with a few minor exceptions, any black South African who is
sufficiently qualified for a given position, will be promoted to
it, and that soon even the few exceptions will be removed. Those
are the pledges and the quite clear and specific impressions
given; are they clearly and undeniably supported by the
facts?

Some years ago, a South African economist who was also
a member of the now-illegal multi-racial South African Liberal
Party, described the racial employment and promotion situation
in South Africa in these terms :

> Take a vertical glass tube. Pour in five cups of water and
> one cup of oil. The oil will float on the top of the water. Now
> on a scale behind the tube mark out a list of jobs graded in
> rewards and responsibility from unskilled labourer at the
> bottom, to Chairman of the Board, Government Minister
> and senior civil servant, etc., at the top. If you now mark
> the dividing line between the oil and the water as "Job
> Reservation", you have a working model of the South African
> employment situation under apartheid. The oil is the whites,
> the water is the blacks—so the whites always stay above the
> blacks. And the dividing line, Job Reservation, can be made
> to adjust to minor variations in the employment situation
> simply by adjusting the scale at the back. But wherever that
> dividing line may be on the job scale, all the whites stay on
> top of all the blacks, just as oil always stays above water.
> For by law, no black may be promoted directly above a white
> in South Africa.

This simple model is, in fact, supported by the racial laws
of South Africa, by ministerial statements, even by the South
African government's propaganda material, and by the very
facts of daily life within South Africa. As follows :

The facts
The innocently named South African Industrial Conciliation
Act, No. 28 of 1956, contains within it a Section 77. This is a

racial clause applicable to all employment in South Africa. It can ensure that while any white in South Africa may employ or supervise any non-white, the converse—as the free world understands it—is forbidden. No non-white may occupy a position of authority over a white, no matter how experienced, educated and talented the non-white, or how junior and inexperienced the white; this is the broad principle involved.

At the same time, allowance was made in the Act for adjusting the marginal jobs between white and black—such as lift operators—by the mechanism of "job determinations". These can be altered simply by ministerial decree, and hundreds have been issued over the years. Their function is to ensure full employment for whites by taking over black jobs in time of unemployment, and letting whites rise to better jobs in boom years. It is this more direct effect of Section 77 which has erroneously taken all the world-wide publicity as Job Reservation.

Section 77 is still in force. And over the years, white South Africans have repeatedly been reassured by their government that it does mean, in practice, that all whites are superior to all non-whites in employment, a typical example being statements made in parliament by the South African Minister of Labour during 1971 alone[4]—fifteen years after the law was promulgated.

On 9 February 1971, the minister said that 2.9 per cent of the total South African labour force was potentially affected by Job Reservation. On 18 May, the same minister plainly admitted that Job Reservation, and legal barriers to the promotion of blacks above whites, were two quite different subjects when he said in parliament: "If Section 77 was to be repealed, that would *not only* undo the two per cent Job Determinations, but the whole statutory pedestal would be wrenched out from under our whole traditional labour policy." What that pedestal was, underpinning Section 77 of the Industrial Conciliation Act, the Minister of Labour made clear on 9 September 1971, when he said in a policy statement: "No white is allowed to work under a non-white in South Africa". In other words, no non-white is allowed to work over a white.

The year after the Industrial Conciliation Act of 1956 was passed, the South African Nursing Act, No. 69 of 1957, became law. In medicine it, too, forbids non-whites from giving orders to whites, and makes them subservient to whites. What this means in practice became clear in a well-publicized case in

1975, when a white theatre nurse in South Africa prohibited an experienced Indian surgeon from performing an operation in a Durban hospital. In law, her skin-colour takes precedence over the doctor's professional position and skills.

The facts of daily life alone in South Africa are therefore sufficient to show that the racial employment laws are indeed all-embracing, and are by no means restricted—as talk about Job Reservation suggests—to only 2.9 per cent of the population. In any given company or its departments in South Africa the racial profile of command and authority is instantly apparent. At the top are the whites, at the bottom are the blacks. Only in the middle is there sometimes some apparent diffusion of the principle of whites above blacks, and this will be found to be a matter of job performance rather than one of authority—for even the most junior white has his right to issue orders to blacks protected in law, one way or another.

True, one does find an occasional well-qualified black employee earning more than some whites in a limited number of companies, but they have, by and large, no intrinsic authority over whites. Further, when positions which would entail direct control of white staff—i.e., nearly all worthwhile positions—fall vacant, non-whites are barred from applying for them, or simply not considered for them.

Thus, while it is possible to find, when looking at the broad spectrum of employment in South Africa, black academics and executives on the one hand and white semi-skilled labourers and office boys on the other, Section 77 still applies,[5] in that in the final analysis the white man is implicitly protected.

The Industrial Conciliation Act and the Nursing Act are not the only laws designed to keep non-whites at a subservient level, regardless of merit, in South African employment. In addition to racial "closed shop" agreements between the white trades unions and most of South Africa's biggest companies in mining, industry and commerce, under which all the higher-paid skilled work is reserved for whites, there is also the Group Areas Act with its multiplicity of amendments. Some of these make it compulsory for persons employed in supervisory or managerial positions in South African commerce to be of the same race as their employers. Since nearly all South African commerce is owned and controlled by whites, anyone who is not racially pure white cannot be promoted to senior positions. The various laws, customs and ministerial orders inter-mesh and lock together to form an impenetrable barrier to general black promotion by merit in South Africa. And in fact, comments by two black South Africans of widely different political views can usefully be viewed in relation to the white-made laws and white pronouncements on the matter.

In a book published in 1977, *South African Economic Issues*, a black South African lecturer at a correspondence college is quoted as stating of his country : "There are no black executive positions in industry—directors, general managers, production managers, etc." Not only is this true, but it is a fact which the South African government would have some difficulty in denying, because its own Department of Information published the book, which its embassies have been distributing throughout the world ever since.

The other black South African is quite well known. Shortly before his arrest and imprisonment without trial in October 1977 for criticizing the South African government, editor Percy Qoboza of *The World* newspaper in Johannesburg wrote in an article : "Government policy makes it impossible for us to acquire high executive positions in industry, because we would then be in senior positions to whites."[6]

If the above statements and laws are a true reflection of the overall racial employment situation in South Africa, then their effects must be instantly observable in South African daily life. And they are. For instance, it seems to have occurred to no one in the higher echelons of British, American and European industry to question why their branches or subsidiary companies in South Africa, a country where non-whites make up 83 per cent of the population, have doubtfully had even one non-white director between them. (There are, in truth, a handful of black directors in South Africa—in non-executive positions in fringe companies such as small publishing firms and so on where some inside knowledge may be necessary.)

Indeed, if one were to represent the racial structure of authority and subservience in a wide range of South African companies and organizations by listing each company's staff vertically, one would find something unique to South Africa— a point in every company or department above which all are white, and below which all are black. If one groups these staff-lists side-by-side and connects each of those transition points, one would have a clear picture of South African employment practices as they really are—all the whites above the line, all the blacks below it. So that Job Reservation could be abolished entirely as promised in May 1979 after the Wiehahn Report and still the blacks would be discriminated against, because "no white is allowed to work under a non-white in South Africa".

This mechanism of preserving total control of the rich South African economy in white hands, while apparently abolishing racial practices such as Job Reservation, has been dealt with at some length because it helps to explain the many official pronouncements on the subject. Perhaps the most fascinating of these has ironically been quoted by a South African embassy official in an attempt to *deny* nation-wide restrictions on black promotion in South Africa.

It will be recalled that South African employers and government sources alike have since early 1977 insisted that they have undertaken to "promote staff without regard to race or colour". Yet on 26 July 1977, the South African Minister of Bantu Administration had "constructive discussions" with the Association of Chambers of Commerce in South Africa (Assocom), as a result of which "Assocom would prepare, at the request of the minister, guidelines for his consideration on the training and appointment of black managers in white urban areas where there was a preponderance of black customers and *a totality of black employees*".[7] (My italics.)

In plain fact, this statement tacitly admits that where there is not a totality of black employees—i.e., where there are white employees who might be junior to a black manager in terms of authority and command—no black managers will be appointed, for this would mean promoting blacks above whites. Yet this directly contradicts the pledges made both by the government and white South African employers that they *would* promote blacks "without regard to race or colour".

The fact is that there is hardly a company in the whole of South Africa where all the employees are black. The guidelines which the white employers were to prepare for the minister, then, would leave racist practices wholly unaffected. Anti-black discrimination in South African employment must thus continue, under the terms of such agreements between white industry and white cabinet ministers, to affect almost 100 per cent of the black people of South Africa, by ensuring that skin whiteness always overrules merit in promotions. And even apart from Section 77, other anti-black laws remain in force.

The Codes of Conduct

At this point, the much-publicized "Codes of Employment Practice" for foreign companies operating in South Africa can usefully be compared with the facts. The codes are claimed to be a means, in the hands of South African-based companies applying them, of ensuring fair employment practices, equal pay for equal work and the opening of all jobs to suitably qualified applicants in South Africa, *regardless of race or colour*.

The American code of practice for US firms operating in South Africa was announced in March 1977. Its principles include equal and fair employment practices for blacks, Coloureds and whites, plus the establishment of training programmes for non-white workers, more management opportunities and better facilities. It contains no clauses specifically challenging the apartheid concept that whites will retain authority over blacks in employment in South Africa, and it totally avoids mention of anti-black laws.

The European Economic Community code for European companies operating in South Africa was debated by EEC countries in September 1977. It contains seven sections, dealing with trade unions, South African Influx Control, and the Pass Laws, minimum pay rates for blacks, equal pay for equal work and promotion by merit, fringe benefits, equal working conditions and annual reports on the working of the code. Section 2 in more detail says that employers should try to "alleviate as much as possible" the Influx Control system, whereby black South Africans—but not white ones—born some distance from the main industrial areas may not live or work there or even bring their wives and families with them without extensive government documentation, which can be cancelled at any time. And the vital Section 4 says that "all jobs should be open to any worker who possesses suitable qualifications, irrespective of racial or other distinction". Yet this key clause in the code is inhibited in South Africa by Section 77, the Group Areas Act and much else, leading the Federation of German Industry to object, not to the toothless nature of the code but to the fact that in order to make it workable it "asked trading companies to disregard the laws of their host country". (The fact that

Section 77 is derived from a German law—Section 3 of the anti-semitic Nazi Nuremberg Laws of 15 September 1935—is a droll commentary on the confusion which exists in German minds on what is really happening in South Africa.)

The British code is in all main respects similar to the EEC code, yet as noted at the head of this chapter, despite the fact that South African law makes it impossible for the code to affect apartheid in any important way, the British government remains convinced that it will "erode apartheid at its foundations" by some as yet unspecified method.

And finally, there is even a home-grown South African code of practice for black employees in that country. It is an illuminating document. Its preamble says that South African employers "believe in the opportunity for men and women to develop themselves to their fullest potential" and the very first clause says the employers will "strive constantly for the elimination of discrimination based on race or colour". But as the preamble to the code notes that all South African employers subscribing to it commit themselves firmly to exercising the code only within the "South African legal framework",[8] it is not surprising that this South African code has already been called the "Barking Dog Code" by a black South African leader, the reference being to the kind of watchdog that barks furiously at an intruder—provided there is a fence between them so high and strong as to in any case prevent the intruder from gaining entry.

The description is perhaps not unfair, for there is another aspect of these codes—one usually stressed in publicity campaigns for them—which also needs mention. If one compares the firm pledges in the codes to "give equal pay for equal work" with the vertical race structure which South African law enforces in employment, it can be seen that there are only a few categories of job in South Africa which are open to both whites and blacks in the same company anyway. So one of the major principles in the codes of practice applies to only a tiny percentage of the total South African work force.

The reaction of the South African government and most white business associations to facts such as those given above is usually to take refuge in the Bantustan theory of "autonomous self-governing black homelands", claiming that in these areas all opportunity is open to blacks, who may there hold positions above whites. In reality, there has already been much trouble in the Transkei over whites refusing to work under blacks, and anyway the argument seems irrelevant if one remembers that almost all industry and commerce, which the black man helped build, is concentrated in white South Africa, and that the entire homelands scheme is in any case profoundly unjust, as shown in a previous chapter. Further, the whole concept of "border industries" is to starve the black "homelands" of industry by siting it just over the border in white South Africa. The black employees troop over the borders daily into factories where the laws of apartheid still apply.

Until the laws that restrict the promotion of blacks above whites—with all that such promotion entails—are revoked and are seen in practice to have been genuinely revoked, so that blacks can as a matter of course hire and fire whites, have white secretaries and hold proper executive positions on the boards of the major South African companies, it seems fair—in view of the deceptive circumstances often pertaining in South Africa—to treat unspecific claims about conditions in unnamed companies with great caution. Exceptions produced for propaganda purposes are far too common in South Africa to be accepted without thorough investigation; not for the sake of denigrating the white people, but for the sake of the black people whose real circumstances have so often over the years been concealed by clever propaganda, some of it even from the lips of collaborating blacks.

In this connection might be mentioned a very recent South African government reaction to exposure of verifiable facts about its racial employment laws. Despite frequent government propaganda claims that "South Africa has nothing to hide", 1978 saw the passing of the "Protection of Business Information Act" by the South African parliament. This Act makes it a criminal offence for the South African subsidiary of any overseas firm to pass on information to sources outside South Africa—including its own head office—about its black wage rates or South African racial employment practices, without the specific permission of the all-white South African government.

The very existence of such a law perhaps speaks for itself about the true extent of racial discrimination throughout the South African economy as it affects promotion, opportunity, training and the degree to which non-white South Africans may share in their country's business life and financial rewards. But it should also be remembered that the existence of such a law means that most information of the type given in this chapter will in future be censored in South Africa, and may not be transmitted to the outside world. In effect, only the white, pro-apartheid voice on this subject will in future be heard from South Africa, by law.

THE BLACK/WHITE INCOME GAP

An excellent example of the power of economic propaganda to mislead and misdirect when addressed to a suitably self-interested audience can be seen in that perennial subject of discussion, the relative earnings of black and white in South Africa. In this case, for many years South Africa has successfully persuaded a large number of the world's leading politicians, industrialists, investment advisers and newspapers to believe three things about the earnings of the black man under apartheid. They are :

1. That the actual income gap between black and white South Africans is not very large, and is in any case steadily decreasing. 2. That the blacks of South Africa have the highest incomes of blacks anywhere in Africa. 3. That continued overseas investment in South Africa demonstrably helps economic realities to break down racial discrimination, and therefore directly helps all blacks.

If these three widely-held beliefs turn out, on close examination, to be untrue, then once again a wide gap will have been established between what is happening in South Africa, and what the West's mass media and even multi-national companies have been saying is happening in South Africa. And once again, the familiar picture will appear of a Western world partly lulled into complacency about an alleged "narrowing racial income gap" in South Africa, while the victims of that gap see it ever widening, and become ever more angry and committed to action; action which in one way or another could wipe out much of the West's billions of pounds and dollars of investment capital in that part of the world.

It is perhaps a measure of the facile nature of South Africa's economic and investment propaganda that when one comes to look at the figures provided for black incomes in South Africa, not only are most of the important ones missing, but little or no distinction is made between "wages", "income" and even "purchasing power".[1] And one government official, even when the terms are properly defined, is quite likely to flatly contradict another, as will be seen later.

The only worthwhile figures to use in assessing the true size of the income gap between black and white in South Africa are those of total black and total white *per capita* incomes on a national basis, because these give a direct indication of average black/white living standards under apartheid. In fact, as is shown later, the practice common even amongst the West's economists of comparing black wages with white wages in South Africa is highly misleading—in favour of apartheid's apologists —because whites annually share in thousands of millions of rands of unearned income from sources barred to blacks through the racial laws created by the whites.

Black and white incomes
Black incomes in South Africa have long been subject to a series of extraordinary exaggerations by the white authorities. For instance, between the mid-1950s and mid-1960s, the records of the South African Bureau of Statistics show that *per capita* white and black wages both roughly doubled. But in 1965 the South African embassy in London was publicly claiming a "fivefold increase" in black wages during those ten preceding years, the government-controlled South African Broadcasting Corporation was claiming a "fivefold increase" in blacks' wages over the preceding seven years,[2] and a year or two later an official South African book, *South African Quiz*, distributed in huge numbers by embassies throughout the world, was stating (page 119) that "the Bantu, making sole use of the existing arbitrary [sic] machinery to negotiate with their employers, have succeeded in raising their wages by six hundred per cent in the past ten years. In the same period South African whites have increased their wages by twenty per cent." That is, black wages had allegedly risen 30 times faster than white wages, when Pretoria's own records showed that both rates were roughly equal, and even the tacitly pro-apartheid *State of South Africa Year Book* was that year admitting that "Bantu real wages have generally risen more slowly than those of whites".

Yet the propaganda apparently works. After a visit to South Africa the following year, 1968, Sir Alec Douglas Home, then senior foreign affairs spokesman for the British Conservative Party, wrote in an article in the London *Sunday Times* (later gratefully republished by the South African government) that in South Africa "African earnings are rising sharply", when in reality they were almost static, in real terms.

The distinguished politician can hardly be blamed, because South Africa appears to alter figures to suit the argument of the moment. Thus on 6 May 1977, the Deputy Head of the South African Department of Information stated in a document issued to British businessmen (and begging for British investment) at the London embassy: "Over the 1972-75 period the earnings in real terms—after allowing for inflation—of the average white South African worker rose *only three per cent*. The average earnings of black, Coloured and Asian workers rose thirty-three per cent."

But only four months later an official of the same department, the Information Attaché at the same South African embassy, wrote in a letter to the London *Financial Times*, referring to exactly the same period and exactly the same type of wages, "In real terms black wages continue to climb at a faster rate than those of whites, the average of which among economically active blacks rose from 1972 to 1975 by ninety-two per cent, compared with *forty-three per cent for whites*."[3] (My italics).

The disparity between the white wage-rise figures is obvious. There is also a disparity in the non-white figures, less obvious but in fact meaning that if the second statement is correct, all South African Coloureds and Asians had astonishingly had their wages cut by more than half between 1972 and 1975. Proof enough that some or all of these "official South African income figures" are fictitious.

It is clear from the above that it is not an easy matter to establish precise figures for *per capita* overall white and black incomes in South Africa, as some of the official sources are given to gross exaggerations. However, more than a decade of attention to this subject has shown that in practice the figures issued by the South African Bureau of Statistics are generally accurate; close approximations can also be made from National Income figures; and the principle of consistency can usually reduce any residual errors to quite a small margin—rarely more than ten or twenty per cent, which is ample for the purpose of comparing black and white incomes, as the gap between them is enormously larger.

This principle also shows up South Africa's official propaganda figures, for, using those already mentioned, it seems one is expected to believe that white wages rose two per cent per annum from 1957 to 1967, jumped seventy per cent in 1968, then dropped to one per cent per annum from 1969 to the present day. Similarly, private South African sources show some inconsistency, as follows:

In 1974 the somewhat evasive Club of Ten—an anonymous group of largely wealthy whites—claimed in one of its frequent advertisements for South Africa that unskilled black wages in South Africa—i.e., the very lowest—started at a minimum of £25.40 (then about 40 rand) a month.

In 1977, the South Africa Foundation gave figures for 1975[4] which in conjunction with black/white income ratios supplied by the Trust Bank suggested that *average* black wages in 1975 were about what the Club of Ten was claiming as *minimum* wages.

In 1976 Consolidated Goldfields sent its British shareholders a document claiming that the average wage for blacks throughout South Africa was about 80 rand (about £50) a month.[5]

And in 1978 the South African embassy in London claimed that excluding mining and agriculture, average black wages in South Africa during 1976 were really more than 110 rands (about £70) a month.[6]

As already remarked, figures for black and white overall incomes *per capita* in South Africa can be satisfactorily assessed from a variety of professional and competent sources mostly unconnected with the South African publicity machine. These can be compared for rationality and consistency over the years, and from them it is easy to assemble a reasonably accurate picture of the actual income gap between white and black, and whether it is increasing or decreasing.

South Africa's Afrikaner Nationalist government, with its policy of so-called "separate development of the races", has been in power since 1948, so to take at least the latter two-thirds of this period as an example of what effect the whites' racial policies are having on black and white incomes is statistically legitimate.

The figures given are from as wide a range of professional authorities as possible, consistent with reliability, in or converted to Rands.

SOUTH AFRICAN BLACK PER CAPITA INCOMES, PER ANNUM

1954, R55 per annum. A thorough examination of total black income for this year by F. P. Spooner, the South African economist, gave a figure of R482 million for a black population at the time of nine million.

1958, R66 per annum. Statement in Parliament by Minister for Bantu Administration in February 1959, quoting Bureau of Statistics assessment.

1960, R78.5 per annum. Market Potential assessment for University of South Africa by P. A. Nel.

1966, R85 per annum. Calculated from figures admitted in government publications, *South Africa in Fact* and *South African Quiz*, and confirmed in *The Economist* (London), 29/6/68.

1968, R82 per annum. National Development and Management Foundation of South Africa, report, 1969.

1968, R90 per annum. Extrapolation from National Domestic Product figure based on assessment method in *The Political Economy of South Africa* by Ralph Horwitz (Wiedenfeld and Nicolson, 1967).

1968, R80 per annum. Dr R. M. Stoker, past Director of the South African Bureau of Statistics, quoted in *Rand Daily Mail* 21/11/68.

1970, R84 per annum. *South African Financial Mail*, 3/7/70, quoting the most reliable figures available to it.

1973, R120 per annum. *South African Financial Mail*, 21/2/75, quoting figures assembled by the Afrikaner bank Senbank, and South African Reserve Bank data.

1974, R135 per annum. Part of a detailed examination of black incomes in many African countries by Professor Jan Sadie, a leading Afrikaner economist at the University of Stellenbosch in South Africa.[7]

1977, R190 per annum. Figure derived from black household incomes assembled by Markinor research group and quoted in advertisement by the South Africa Foundation in 1978.[8]

These figures are very much lower than the impression given by almost all the more heavily publicized sources, including government propaganda, but this is partly due to two sometimes unsuspected causes. The first is that the just-quoted figures are *per capita*, whereas the publicists prefer to quote so-called "average" wages; that is, the total black wage bill divided not by the total black population, but by the one-third that is economically active.

The second cause is that the "average" wages quoted usually turn out, on inspection, to be not average at all, but the wages of blacks in the best-paid jobs such as government service, commerce, construction and industry (see, for instance, the wage figures sent to enquirers by the Trust Bank of South Africa after advertising in the West's press in 1973). Yet the South African government itself (e.g., in *South African Quiz*) admits that such wage-earners make up only about the top fifteen per cent of black South African earners. What has been omitted is the much lower wage-levels of the rest—labourers, domestic servants and the like.

In fact, during the 1972 period reliable sources such as the Bureau of Market Research and the Johannesburg *Financial Mail* pointed out that black labourers on white farms numbered more than a million, and earned little more than R5 a month for casual labourers to R16 a month for those on the richest white farms (in sterling, some £3 to £9 a month).[9] So the ill-paid majority brings the average per wage-earner down to less than R300 per annum, or about R90 *per capita*; around R7.50 a month, in 1973.

But the full story of the black/white income gap was told in the *Financial Mail* on 21 February 1975. Quoting figures assembled by Senbank, an Afrikaans merchant bank, combined with Bureau of Statistics data and official property and transfer-income figures, Senbank was able to produce Disposable Personal Income figures for all race groups with a percentage error "so small as to be negligible". These carefully assembled figures follow :[10]

Salaries and wages: total R9,557 million.
    Whites 68.2%   Blacks 21.1%   Coloureds 7.9%   Asians 2.8%
Income from property: total R3,161 million.
    Whites 98.1%   Blacks 0.0%   Coloureds 0.3%   Asians 1.6%
Transfers from government: total R418 million.
    Whites 69.8%   Blacks 23.0%   Coloureds 3.6%   Asians 3.6%
Disposable Personal Income: R12,187 million.
    Whites 73.9%   Blacks 17.2%   Coloureds 6.4%   Asians 2.5%[10]

To which information can usefully be added the actual percentages of each race which make up the total population of South Africa:

Whites 17%   Blacks 71%   Coloureds 9%   Asians 3%

There is some corroboration from an unusual source of this large disparity in black and white incomes. In the London *Financial Times* of 27 January 1978, the South African embassy stated that the share of all non-white South Africans in the Net National Income "increased from 26 per cent in 1960 to 32 per cent in 1975". Subtracting the higher-paid Asians' and Coloureds' 10.5 per cent share, this means the black (African) share of the national income was no more than 21.5 per cent for 1975. Thus even the South African authorities themselves have openly if perhaps unwittingly admitted, in view of the population figures given above, that the average black South African gets less than one-thirteenth the annual income of the average white South African, per head.

Two further points need to be made. The Senbank figures show up a fact well known within South Africa, but lacking in all the overseas mass media's reports, news items and articles about South Africa: that in effect black South Africans are barred by the whites from participating in the lucrative property market of their own country—whereas the whites' *per capita* income from property alone in South Africa is *more than five times black per capita incomes from all sources,* as can be seen below. (In 1973, four million whites shared more than R3,000 million from property—R750 per white man, woman and child.) The *Financial Mail* then calculated average annual *per capita* incomes for 1973 as:

Whites: R2,200 Blacks: R120 Coloureds: R350 Asians: R445

That is, white incomes average about eighteen times black incomes, per head.

As white incomes are rather easier to assess (two sources are correlated below) it is now possible to compare annual *per capita* incomes for white and black, and the two income graphs appear on page 114. For the record, the white *per capita* income figures used are as follows, across a wide scatter of years:

SOUTH AFRICAN WHITE ANNUAL INCOMES, PER CAPITA

	Calculated from Net National Income	Independent spot figures
1956	R775	—
1961	R885	R860*
1964	R1,100	—
1968	R1,400	R1,450**
1970	R1,600	—
1973	R2,350	R2,200***
1976	R3,400	—

(* South African Minister of Finance, 15/2/61. ** Past Director of the South African Bureau of Statistics, *Rand Daily Mail*, 21/11/68. *** Senbank.)

The Income gap

As noted earlier in this chapter, one of the most consistent claims by white South African officials and those whom they have persuaded to accept their unsubstantiated figures—including many of the great names in world finance and industry—is that the gap between black and white incomes is narrowing all the time. The graph shows that this is not so. And there is another means by which to test this particular claim.

This is by the comparison of household incomes, because the average number of persons per household varies only very slightly within each racial group—although black households are usually larger than white, thus accounting for the apparently better black-income performances when assessed by households.

Various issues of the *South African Financial Mail*, e.g., 24 January 1975 and 17 February 1976, have carried household-income figures over the years from reputable sources such as Market Research Africa Limited. They show quite clearly that from 1962 to 1973, the income disparity between black and white households, far from narrowing, practically doubled. The size of the gap also widened from the average white household having R362 more to spend per month than the average black household in 1970, to R546 more for whites than blacks in 1975. An ever-increasing gap consistent with individual income disparities.

The "richest blacks in Africa"?

One of the best-known—and most believed—of white South Africa's claims concerning the black South Africans' financial

Annual *per capita* incomes (see text) to the same scale
(In early 1979, R100 = £60 or US $120 approx.)

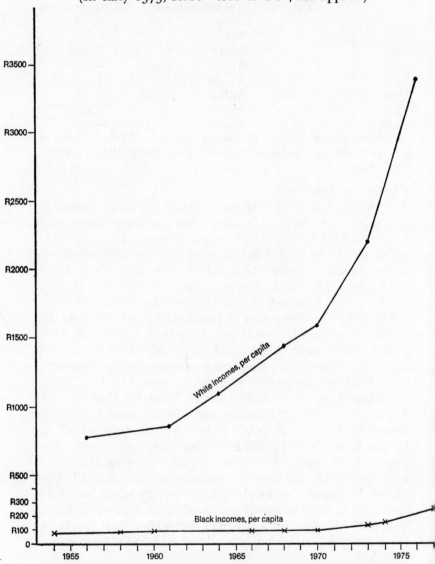

N.B. To allow for government claims that some 15 per cent
should be added to black incomes to account for white help to
blacks and their "homelands", a full 20 per cent has been
added to all black incomes to avoid any possible underestimation.

situation under apartheid is that the blacks have the highest incomes of blacks anywhere in Africa—or, as a senior British Conservative MP put it in a newspaper article in London on 16 March 1976: "South Africa...has the healthiest, best educated and most prosperous black population in the continent".

There is much reason to doubt this claim. A thorough investigation in 1969 showed that at least six black-ruled states in Africa provided higher *per capita* incomes for their black inhabitants than did South Africa—by far the wealthiest state per *overall* population in Africa, and so with a high cost of living as well. *The South African Connection* (Temple Smith, 1972) raised this to thirteen states paying their blacks better than South Africa, and the leading Afrikaner economist Jan Sadie, Professor of Economics at Stellenbosch University in the Cape, assessing *per capita* incomes throughout Africa, put South Africa's blacks not first, but thirteenth (*Rand Daily Mail*, Johannesburg, 2 February 1975).

Of considerable significance is the fact, according to figures quoted by the Afrikaner merchant bank Mercabank ("Focus on Key Economic Issues", 1975) that at that time the Gross National Product of South Africa was about three times that of Zambia, *per capita*—but that the average black Zambian annual income was, at R231, considerably above that of black South Africans at R135.

Such facts are readily obtainable from authoritative sources throughout the world, and speak for themselves both of the true nature of apartheid and of the veracity of the extensive South African-originated propaganda which flatly contradicts these financial facts and attempts to claim exactly the opposite. Indeed, the level of responsibility of such propaganda is easily tested by a popular South African claim published, *inter alia,* in the official government booklet "Progress Through Separate Development", which on page 28 made the statement that South Africa's non-whites represent "the wealthiest non-white nation" in the world. As their *per capita* income at the time was barely more than £50 per annum, one noted economist commented that apparently the South African government had never heard of Japan.

The plea for "continued investment to help the blacks"
By far the most common argument used by South Africa—and

by overseas companies with profitable investments in South
Africa—to encourage further investment and prevent with-
drawals of existing investments, is the claim that increased
overseas financial and industrial involvement in South Africa
cannot fail to benefit the blacks, and will even "undermine
apartheid".

This popular white argument is heavily endorsed by South
Africa's publicity machine, both government and private.
"Rising standards of living are head and shoulders above the
rest of Africa and the Bantu population is sharing in them to
the full" encouraged the South African government's London
embassy in its official monthly magazine *Report from South
Africa* in February 1969. Eight years later a senior Department
of Information official was even more direct when he addressed
this message to a seminar of British businessmen interested in
investing in South Africa : "My message to you is simply : to
do business with South Africa is not only profitable, but also
defensible on moral, political and social grounds. The decent
thing to do is not to disengage, but to engage more convincingly, to further help advance the interests of the black and
brown peoples of South Africa." [11]

But although in the last ten years British investment alone
has at least tripled in South Africa, there appears to be no
evidence at all that this has helped to narrow the white/black
income gap. Instead, all the evidence suggests that the gap has
not narrowed at all, but widened tremendously, even though
this is to some extent due to inflation. Senbank's exhaustive
analysis, for instance, makes it clear that black wage increases
would have to be quite astronomical before the black income
line in the graph on page 114 would even begin to parallel the
white line. And this would still not narrow the gap, but leave
it static. And so once again, the propaganda and the facts
about South Africa are seen to be irreconcilable.

But the propaganda continues, often in unusual guises. For
instance, on 25 October 1978 the South African Minister for
Plural Relations stated that "white South Africans deserve the
Nobel Prize for the R600 million they have given to South
Africa's developing black homelands". This statement is another
version of one which says (as quoted from the *South Africa
Official Yearbook*, 1975) that South Africa's "current develop-
ment programme for its black citizens is *per capita*, in terms of

white taxpayers' contributions, the world's largest sustained foreign aid project". (This quote by South Africa's London embassy is particularly interesting because it defines black South Africans both as South African citizens and as foreigners: an example of propaganda "double-think".)

In reality, South African economists have themselves pointed out that cheap black labour in South Africa, being the direct cause of low white taxation and low prices for labour-intensive goods and services, actually puts several hundred rands each year in the pockets of every white. And the blacks themselves have repeatedly complained that this alleged (and often unwanted) "aid" must be set against the fact that blacks in South Africa "earn black man's wages, but have to pay white man's prices". A fact mentioned nowhere in South African "information" material.

Further, it is not only white and black South African wage figures which cannot be trusted when they come from South African embassies and other pro-apartheid sources. Volume 12, No. 2 of the South African embassy's (London) glossy monthly magazine *Report from South Africa* carried some emphatic claims about the wages of Coloured (mixed race) South Africans.

In 1973/4, said the magazine, Coloured skilled labourers' "weekly wages varied between R60 and R80", "matriculated Coloureds receive salaries of between R180 and R200 per month when they start working", and so on. The embassy magazine justified these figures with the specific claim that "the Coloureds' share of national spending power surpasses sixteen per cent and is nearing twenty per cent".

But the South African Bureau of Statistics figures for that very same period showed that the wage figures given by the embassy had been exaggerated at least twice, and University of South Africa and Senbank figures showed that the Coloureds' share of national spending power, far from being between sixteen and twenty per cent, was for that year exactly 6.5 per cent.[12]

Footnote on Job Reservation: On 1.5.79 the South African government announced acceptance of the Wiehahn Report on black employment. Hailed by the West's media as "the end of job discrimination", it in fact preserves exactly those "closed shop" practices which keep blacks below whites.

CHAPTER FIVE

Apartheid in Medicine, Education and Sport

MEDICINE, EDUCATION AND sport in South Africa are subjects about which there has been a great deal of often acrimonious controversy for many years. It is not intended here to devote a great deal of space to even more argument on these subjects. Instead, the opportunity will be taken to set down certain essential facts usually hidden by South Africa or ignored by the West. Indeed, much of the West's reporting and comment on these three aspects of South African life appears to have been based on side issues and false trails. In sport, incidentally, such reporting has been particularly marked by the giving of far more publicity to white sportsmen defending the *status quo*, than to non-white South African sportsmen who are or have been the victims of that *status quo*. (This omission is all the greater in view of the fact that non-white and non-racist sports leaders in South Africa have usually been denied passports, thus preventing them from stating their case for themselves.)

MEDICINE

It is not unusual throughout the world to find that the poor, who are in most need of it, actually get a lower level of medical care than the rich. That—by and large—the poor in South Africa are black and the rich are white, so that medicine appears to have a racial tinge, could well be claimed to be a function of apartheid rather than of medicine itself. But in fact the South African government strongly denies that there is any difference in the treatment and medical services available to black patients and white ones. Examples: "All the health services are available to all the inhabitants of the Republic, irrespective of race, colour or religion." ("Health Services in South Africa" in *Report from South Africa, 1975/3-4,* page 9, published by the South Africa embassy, London.) And:

"Patients of all races receive the same treatment." (*Report from South Africa* Vol. 12 No. 5.)

The veracity of such statements is easily enough tested against the known fact that nearly all medical practice in South Africa is segregated by law. Baragwanath Hospital in Soweto is for blacks only. The dozens of modern hospitals and nursing homes in Johannesburg itself are for whites only. Even ambulances must be either "black" or "white"—and occasionally it is the whites instead of the blacks who suffer: when a white child was badly injured in a Johannesburg street in 1975 the ambulance service was told that a "boy" had been hurt, and, as blacks are usually called "boys", a black ambulance was sent. This was not allowed to carry a white, so the child was left on the street and bled to death before a white ambulance could be sent.

Misleading claims abound in South African literature on medical services under apartheid, but several facts central to the controversy should be sufficient to reveal the truth, and expose the propagandists' methods.

Foremost among these facts is the actual number of doctors available to white and black South Africans, on a *per capita* basis (official apartheid legislation ensures that such figures can be quite accurately arrived at as few South African doctors have both black and white patients).

The figures required will, however, be found nowhere in the quite extensive official literature on South African medicine and health services. Instead, an overall figure is usually given—that of roughly one doctor per 2,000 people in South Africa. This claim—which is true as far as it goes—is usually coupled with a reminder that such a figure "proves" that South Africans of "all races" get more extensive medical care than the peoples of any other nation in Africa.

However, it is when the actual number of doctors available to each race group under the strict policy of apartheid is revealed, that the full truth emerges. For official figures show that *per capita*, in South Africa there is one doctor per 450 whites, and one doctor per 11,000 blacks.[1] The discriminatory ratio against blacks in availability of skilled medical help is thus shown by the government's own figures to be more than twenty to one. And apartheid ensures that such discrimination will remain. It is against facts like these that both the true nature of apartheid, and the massive publicity surrounding South Africa's highly sophisticated specialist medical achievements such as heart-transplant surgery, should perhaps be more commonly assessed. And to give credit where it is due, this very point has been made over a period of years by some South African doctors themselves.

For instance, Dr Rodney Hewitson, addressing the South African Academy of Science and Art in Cape Town in 1969, made specific reference to Dr Phillip Blaaiberg's heavily publicized acquisition of a new heart at Groote Schuur Hospital the previous year with the statement: "Two hundred sick and underfed infants could have been kept alive for a year with the money spent on Dr Blaaiberg's operations—a total of £8,927."[2] At about the same time, medical comment overseas was being made on a surprisingly little-known aspect of South Africa's heart-transplant operations. This was that as South African law in effect allows whites to operate on any racial group but forbids black doctors from touching whites or even dissecting white corpses,[3] then South Africa's pioneering heart transplants, all of which involved whites as donor or recipient, might not have legally been performed if Dr Barnard had happened to be black. The point is not critical of Dr Barnard in any way, as he did not make such laws, but it speaks volumes for the kind of basic racial fact about apartheid in medicine in South Africa which rarely if ever comes to public attention outside South Africa, and yet which instantly illuminates the true nature of that policy.

The reference to "sick and underfed infants" touches on another aspect of black health under apartheid which is of undoubted importance, yet which is also rarely mentioned. This is the actual size of the infant-mortality rate (IMR) amongst black South Africans. Where government literature is concerned, the possibility that apartheid-caused malnutrition might take a heavy toll of young black lives is either ignored with statements such as "figures for blacks are unavailable" or shrugged off—"We have only a few cases of malnutrition," said a senior South African official on British television in 1974.[4] But in fact a broad investigation was carried out into this subject between 1970 and 1973, by the simple expedient—which seems not to have occurred to the large number of newspapers reporting on South Africa—of writing to South African Medical Officers of Health and asking for the black IMR figures from their annual reports. (Infant-mortality rate is based on the number of infants per 1,000 live births who die in the first year of life.)

Almost all MOHs replied, with IMR figures for blacks ranging from 68 per 1,000 for Johannesburg in 1968, through 188 per 1,000 for Grahamstown in 1970, to 170 per 1,000 in Bloemfontein in 1972 : the average being well over 120 per 1,000.

However, these figures are for urban areas, where black pay and medical services are both at their best. Surveys in rural areas have shown figures up to 100 per cent higher. Extrapolation of the figures to cover all black South Africans, using as a guide the known IMR at that time of some 130 per 1,000 for the much better paid Coloured people of South Africa, together with data from professional, local research at the time—such as that of E. Kraayenbrink[5]—produces an overall black infant-mortality rate of well in excess of 150 per 1,000 live births for South Africa. The white figure is very accurately known and for the same period averaged 20 per 1,000—less than one-seventh the black rate. Since the black IMR for several much poorer but black-ruled states, such as Ghana, was at the time considerably less than 150 per 1,000, there appears to be no doubt that apartheid is nothing like as beneficial to black South Africans as is often claimed, for the IMR is a classic indicator of living standards.

Where actual numbers are concerned, South African census figures and vital statistics show an annual black birth-rate of some 700,000. Even using the minimal IMR figure of 150 per 1,000, this suggests that at least 100,000 black South African babies die each year. But in Ghana, a quite thorough investigation in the 1960s produced an IMR figure of close to 110 per 1,000, an IMR which if applied to South Africa would result in the saving of the lives of at least 30,000 black infants every year.

Even this cautious figure—the toll paid by black babies for apartheid, in effect—suggests that about half a million needless black infant deaths have occurred in South Africa since 1960, the year of the Sharpeville massacre which caused 69 black deaths. These 69 deaths made worldwide news largely because they were violent deaths. The probable half million totally unnecessary infant deaths since, presumably because they were non-violent—yet doubtless just as agonizing—have been subject to a blanket of general silence.

Where the facts are even partly admitted, it is claimed that the high IMR is really the blacks' own fault because it is due to "the traditionally wrong eating habits of the Bantu"—a reason denied by historians and archaeologists who point out that before the white man came most blacks enjoyed "a rich and varied diet".[6] The real cause of a high infant-mortality rate is lack of money, education and doctors—and in the case of South Africa's black population all these factors are under the strict control of the white minority.

(In fairness, it should be mentioned that the Medical Association of South Africa several years ago publicly denied that the black IMR was even as high as that for the much better paid Coloured community. But it made no attempt to explain how this extraordinary medical paradox could come about, ignored almost all the official black IMR figures given here, which strongly contradict its statements, and at one point actually contradicted itself: as quoted by its London embassy. In fact, extensive fieldwork by the South African Institute of Race Relations supports a high black IMR figure.)

Some space has been devoted here to the subject of black South African infant-mortality rates for two reasons. The first is that the cautious estimate of more than 30,000 black South African babies suffering and dying from the inequalities of apartheid every year is a figure which needs to be compared, in all humanity, with the figure of only a few hundred white Rhodesians who have died at the hands of black guerrillas in that country over the past ten years. Many of these white deaths, tragic as they are, have been massively publicized throughout the world, while the equally agonizing mass deaths of multitudes of black babies in South Africa (and Rhodesia) caused by white racial discrimination has remained largely unreported, and indeed energetically denied with official statements which fly in the face of professionally gathered medical facts.

The second reason is that the black South Africans are themselves asking how much longer their children are expected to die in their thousands, while the whites only slowly come to grips with such problems because of "the necessity to face-

save"—to quote indirectly from a South Africa Foundation
statement in *To The Point* (7 July 1978). This phrase is preceded in the Foundation's statement with the comment, referring to possible improvements in black South Africans' life
styles, that "A degree of Western patience is needed". Yet
fifteen years earlier in the *Reader's Digest* an American VIP
who had recently been a guest of a white South African group
had written an article "Why South Africa needs time", pleading for the West to move slowly over fighting apartheid. In the
intervening fifteen years, possibly more than 400,000 black
babies have died from apartheid-caused malnutrition. Yet the
whites' plea is always the same: "We need more time"—or to
quote from the same page of *To The Point,* mentioned above,
"Changes . . . cannot be hurried without violence and destruc-
tion"—said a titled Briton at a lavish dinner, referring to the
race situation in South Africa.

(To yet another hungry and grief-stricken black South
African family, burying yet another child dead from malnutrition in a country which exports vast quantities of food, such
statements must at best seem totally meaningless. "Violence,"
said a black South African now imprisoned for criticizing the
government, "means suffering and death. Apartheid means
suffering and death. But at least violence comes to an end,
while apartheid goes on for ever; unless we stop it with
violence.")

One more point on this subject: many churchmen, both
inside and outside South Africa, have drawn back from even
remotely condoning violence on the part of the oppressed, in
the honest hope that prayer and persuasion will eventually
change the hearts of the oppressors. But if the above infant-
death figures have any validity at all, then each day gained
for a policy of non-violence sees the deaths of yet another 100
innocent black babies in South Africa; a terrible dilemma for
genuine Christians, yet one which they must, eventually, face
in all its implications.

As in most other aspects of South African propaganda
defending apartheid, racial discrimination in medicine is disguised by the misuse of statistics coupled with false analogies.
As noted earlier, on both the official and the private level it is
popularly claimed that South Africa has one doctor for every
2,000 of the population. In official government books such as

the full-colour, 120-page *Health and Healing* (Department of Information, Pretoria), this figure is then compared with the doctor/population ratio for certain selected black-ruled states in Africa, to the detriment of all such black states. (This is one of the many ways in which South African publicity material persistently—and falsely—denigrates black Africa.)

But the comparison is, of course, not valid. Elsewhere in Africa, doctors of all races may treat patients of all races, whereas South Africa's race policies ensure that for the black majority there is one doctor, not for 2,000 but for 11,000 persons. Figures given in *Health and Healing* showing one doctor for 5,700 people in Gabon and one doctor for 8,900 people in Zambia, compared with "one per 2,000" for South Africa, thus pervert the truth. For in fact, blacks in Gabon and Zambia, both much poorer states *per capita* than South Africa, actually have better access to medical services than do the blacks of South Africa, at one doctor per 11,000 blacks—an official figure.

Apartheid in medicine has other disastrous effects on black health. It is rarely understood outside South Africa that, for instance, the discrimination of five to one against blacks in the number of hospital beds available means more than just four times more beds for whites, *per capita,* than for blacks. Because of the very nature of apartheid itself, it means that if a black hospital is full to overflowing (as they usually are), sick and injured blacks unable to gain admission cannot simply be sent across to a white hospital with empty beds, perhaps only a mile or two away. For that would contravene white South Africa's apartheid laws. Beds in white hospitals will therefore remain empty, while the waiting black patients are either sent home or transferred by second-class ambulance perhaps 100 miles or more to a black hospital which might be able to take them. There are exceptions to this practice—Groote Schuur Hospital in Cape Town is one—but this is how apartheid works in practice for most black South Africans in need of hospitalization.

Such figures are actually worse than they seem, because high levels of malnutrition amongst blacks in South Africa not only produce deficiency diseases unknown amongst the white population, but also induce a low level of general health. Yet as noted earlier, South Africa denies that such malnutrition exists.

For instance, the people of Britain were told by the South

African embassy in 1972 that South Africa "is in a position where undernourishment is not a problem".[7] Exactly a year later the *South African Medical Journal* noted that a survey of black children in the Transvaal, South Africa's wealthiest province, had revealed that almost three-quarters of those living in rural areas and the poorer urban townships were technically suffering from mild to moderate malnutrition. Two months later a Johannesburg paediatrician stated that more than 60 per cent of all black children admitted for whatever reason to Soweto's sole hospital had to be treated for malnutrition as a medical necessity.[8] There is much other professional material over the years directly contradicting almost all South African government claims for black health and welfare. Yet one more point about black malnutrition perhaps needs to be mentioned here, in view of its long-term implications.

This is that apartheid may well be condemning many thousands of black South Africans to a semi-vegetable existence, through retardation of brain growth and defective intellectual development caused by malnutrition during infancy. Those black babies whose malnutrition is not sufficiently severe to turn them into infant-mortality-rate statistics may thus become another, perhaps grimmer kind of statistic. And one which rarely, if ever, applies to South African whites.

Much of the early work—whose validity is now confirmed—on this subject was performed in the 1960s by Drs Mavis Stock and Patrick Smythe. Their research project encompassed large numbers of undernourished and malnourished infants. Yet this real contribution to medical knowledge is never mentioned in South African propaganda material—even though it was carried out in South Africa. For it was black and Coloured South African infants who provided the evidence.

EDUCATION

Black education

The subject of black education in South Africa is one that suddenly leapt to the attention of the world in 1976, when substantial numbers of protesting black schoolchildren in Soweto and elsewhere were shot dead by the South African police. Considerable news coverage was given to the final straw which broke the black children's patience—the refusal of their all-white government even to consider their request to abandon a Bantu education system under which the initial years of a black child's education were conducted in his tribal language (which many do not know) but the more advanced classes were taught some subjects in English, and the rest in Afrikaans.

World surprise at a system which forces blacks to be fluent in three different languages in order to understand their school-lessons, while their white compatriots need to be fluent in only one, was increased by the fact that not a whisper of this dis-criminatory and indeed inflammatory state of affairs had appeared in any of the large numbers of books, booklets and pamphlets issued by South Africa in praise of Bantu education. Instead, white South Africa's publicity material was carrying eulogies about the "phenomenal achievements in the field of black education", and the few actual figures given were such that it was impossible to discover the real point at issue—the difference between white education and black education in the same country.

Since few of the public media in the West have carried the most pertinent figures of all—the relative *per capita* amounts spent annually on white and black education in South Africa—and since South African "information" material only rarely gives these figures, and then never in a form which allows them to be compared with each other, they are given here at intervals from the time Bantu Education was introduced by the present white régime in 1953 :

Year	Expenditure per white child	Expenditure per black child	Discriminatory ratio against blacks
1953	R100	R18	$5\frac{1}{2}$: 1
1963	R140	R12.50	11 : 1
1972	R220	R20	11 : 1
1974	R470	R29	16 : 1

(Sources: Bureau of Statistics, Pretoria (1953); *Rand Daily Mail* articles by leading South African educationalists, published 31 August and 21 September 1965 (1953 and 1963); *Report from South Africa*, South African Department of Information (1963); *Cape Argus*, Cape Town, 7 May 1975, *The Guardian*, London, 27 May 1975, and South African embassy official on BBC-TV, 12 December 1974 (1974).)

Although some published figures for 1975 suggest a slight widening of the education expenditure gap to $16\frac{1}{2}$ to 1 against black children, reliable later figures have proved difficult to obtain, apparently because of an information barrier erected after the Soweto school violence from 1976 onwards. However in parliament on 18 February 1976, figures were given showing that as in so many other aspects of apartheid, the "brown" races fare considerably better than the blacks, but still worse than the whites. Indian South African children in 1975 had R170 *per capita* spent on their education, and Coloured South African children R125; discriminatory ratios compared with white children of roughly three to one and four to one respectively, in favour of the whites.

The figures above are particularly important precisely because they are overall *per capita* figures which accurately describe the degree of discrimination against blacks in South African education over the country as a whole. Far too many propagandists, both pro-apartheid and anti-apartheid, have preferred to illustrate the whole situation of black/white education in South Africa by selecting a few schools and suggesting that these are typical of all. The worst offenders are, it seems, the South African pro-apartheid whites—one large privately printed book which was sent unsolicited to schools and politicians in many overseas countries including in its wide range of colour illustrations only the very best black schools and colleges, and only the best-dressed black children. (The book also contained the official, false version of South African history.)

In fact, there are many modern, well-equipped black educational institutions in South Africa. But they are only a tiny percentage of the whole and few even of the best can compare with white schools and colleges. Much more typical—because more black children attend them—are farm schools, for the children of white South Africa's black farm labourers. Often nothing but huts built by unpaid black labour, their black teachers are usually paid only a few rands a month, equipment is minimal or completely lacking, and the white farmer has the power to decide which black children should attend, who shall teach there and even if there is to be a school at all. The South African government itself has described the purpose of such schools—now attended by more than 400,000 black children— as "teaching the black child in order to fit him for farm work".[9] The system is largely identical to that in America's "Deep

South" a century ago, with the children committed to farm labour for life.

As in the case of black wages, much publicity material from South Africa compares black education in that country favourably with black education in black-ruled states elsewhere in Africa, but never with white education in South Africa. Even so, figures are rarely given and, when the researcher uncovers them and compares the facts, the South African claims are usually found to be false.

One example: in the official Department of Information book, *Multinational Development in South Africa: the Reality* (1974), is the statement that "In standard and scope the education programmes for South Africa's black peoples have no equal in black Africa". No figures are given in support of this claim. However, in the previous year H. Lewis Jones in *Free Southern Africa* (May 1973) had given the latest available comparative figures against which such claims can be tested. He noted that black pupils in secondary schools as a percentage of total black school population in 1969/70 worked out as 4.2 per cent for South Africa, seven per cent for Zambia and nine per cent for Kenya. As the overall Kenyan percentage of black children at school is not far below South Africa's, and the Zambian percentage is much the same, South Africa's claim is disproved. Even if one takes Total Expenditure on Education as a proportion of Gross National Product (probably the fairest comparison), both Kenya and Zambia come out well above South Africa, the wealthiest state by far on the African continent.

As for the nature of black education in South Africa, despite the massive disparity of some sixteen to one against black children in expenditure, official documents such as the government's *Bantu Education Journal* repeatedly make claims such as "education is basically the same for all races" in South Africa. The year after this particular claim, the South African Department of Labour's *Manpower Survey* (No. 10, 27 April 1973) revealed the effects of this "basically the same" education. There were then 10,038 white engineers in South Africa—and one black engineer. 8,444 white doctors—and 69 black doctors. 1,052 white dentists and two black dentists. And 1,856 white architects—and no black architects at all. And all this twenty years after the introduction of the Bantu Education Act, at which time the government had promised that very soon "thousands" of black graduates pouring from new black universities would "completely vindicate" apartheid in education.

What black South Africans are actually taught under an education system wholly controlled by the white-minority government is a matter too wide-ranging to more than hint at here, but an indication of the complete political control of black education can be glimpsed from the fact that under the Bantu Education Act of 1953, it is an offence for anyone who is not a teacher approved by the state to teach a black person anything academic at all. (South African legal authorities have long pointed out that this even means that a white housewife teaching her black cook to read is breaking the law.) The result of such laws is that anything touching on history, race or politics must be taught to black South Africans in a manner strictly conforming to government policy on such matters. For instance, it has long been known that only the false, government-created version of South Africa's racial history may legally be taught to black children, and it was partly due to a cumulative revulsion by pupils and teachers alike against such racial distortions that the Soweto eruption in 1976 came, when it did, from the schools.

Yet the schools themselves are only a part of the overall system of indoctrination to which the black majority in South Africa is subject. Bantu Radio, broadcasting mainly in the local African languages, is politically controlled by the white government. Draconian film censorship for blacks by the same government removes almost all films but cops-and-robbers, Westerns and an occasional musical from the screens of black cinemas (film censorship in South Africa varies according to the race of the audience, but all censoring is done by whites). And with the change to Frequency Modulation in internal radio services and government encouragement for the manufacture of cheap sets for blacks without short-wave or AM bands, nearly all black radio listeners are restricted to line-of-sight transmissions, from their own country's transmitters. The criteria for mass isolation and indoctrination of the black majority are thus almost wholly fulfilled, and have some quite exact parallels to many Communist states, and even to Nazi Germany.

And, of course, all education in South Africa—with the exception of a handful of university courses affecting only a few hundred blacks—is racially segregated. The point is stressed because of some recent interesting omissions in information originating from South Africa. One example should suffice.

In its regular page in the South African magazine *To The Point International* on 23 January 1978, a South African organization published an article titled "Furthering Black Education", praising the University of South Africa (UNISA). In passages such as "UNISA stands as a truly outstanding example of multi-racial transnational institution" . . . "More than a quarter of the students are black, Indian or Coloured" and so on, the article gives an impression of all races in South Africa happily mixing in lectures and on the campus of a typical university. What the article does not mention is that the University of South Africa strictly observes the laws of apartheid because it is in fact a correspondence college. Most students of this "multi-racial institution" never meet each other.

White education

Much of the education available to whites in South Africa is of a very high standard, but subjects touching on politics and race show similar distortions to the government's propaganda themes—e.g., approved text-books for both white and black South African schools carry much of the false version of South African history, and/or omit events and facts showing Afrikaner Nationalism in a bad light. Perhaps the most significant aspect of white education is that which was actually filmed during the making of the British ATV documentary *The South African Experience* in 1977 : the general indoctrination of white children in South Africa's schools into the belief that whites are innately superior as a race, and blacks innately inferior and suitable only for menial and labouring tasks. This deliberate teaching of racism in white South African schools is a factor which cannot be ignored in any assessment of South Africa's future prospects for peace, or racial civil war.

APARTHEID IN SPORT

Of all the many aspects of apartheid, that which has received most international attention and roused most controversy and even violence over the years would appear to be the racial nature of South African sport. Yet this form of apartheid is clearly one of the least important, especially when compared with the often lethal results of apartheid in medicine, or the long-term crippling of black aspirations and opportunities caused by apartheid in education.

The attention given to apartheid in sport seems to derive from two factors—emotionalism and tactics. Emotionally, within South Africa the average white sportsman—and especially the rugby player—has unconsciously elevated sport into a symbol of white virility and superiority, to such a degree that in 1964 the government-controlled South African Broadcasting Corporation actually cancelled a radio broadcast of a championship "white" golf match when it was learned that a brown South African had been given permission to take part. Tactically, overseas groups which object to apartheid have found the "whites only" nature of South African sporting teams an excellent way in which both to protest against apartheid in general and to draw attention to its visibly unjust nature.

The overall facts of apartheid in sport are well-enough known —the originally "all-white" composition of all South African teams, the steady exclusion of such racially-chosen teams from international competition, the slow inclusion by the whites of a few non-whites in national teams, while denying that this had been caused by international pressure, and the repeated assurances at every stage that (to quote one of the latest) "sport has been normalized on a non-racial basis in South Africa".

However, as in almost every other aspect of international comment on apartheid, some of the more crucial points about apartheid in sport—which might well have helped reduce the controversy from its often vituperative and even hysterical level —have been repeatedly glossed over.

For instance, few if any commentators seem to have noticed that sport is the one area in which none of the usual excuses for apartheid hold good. By any sporting criterion, any black man born in South Africa is entitled to represent the country of his birth if he is good enough. Education, literacy, tribe, social customs and all the other apologias used by white South Africa for various forms of apartheid are irrelevant where sport is concerned. So sport is not just a situation where a *prima facie* case of clear anti-black racism is proved against white South Africa every time blacks are excluded from the trials for any of South Africa's local or national cricket, rugby, tennis, water-polo and other teams. It has also produced a new set of excuses for excluding blacks which by their very nature give strong clues to the real depth of racial feeling amongst South African whites, at the same time as their propagandists say to the world such things as: "We white South Africans recognize the black man as a fellow human being".

Excuses for the lack of blacks in prestigious and often profitable sporting events in South Africa and overseas have ranged from the biologically untrue 1968 claim by a senior white sporting official to an American journalist, that blacks are "not suited" to swimming because "the water closes their pores and they cannot get rid of carbon dioxide, so they tire quickly",[10] to the statement by a young Australian surfing champion in 1975 who said he had been assured by his white South African hosts that the reason for the all-white composition of the South African surf life-saving team was that coloured people didn't go near the water "because they consider the surf a voodoo area".

Similar major gaps between fact and claim have been seen over the years in a variety of expensive advertisements placed by white South Africa in attempts to regain admission to the Olympic Games. One such, from the South African government itself in 1975, carried the headline "Could the next Olympics be in Pretoria, South Africa?" and was published in many important newspapers throughout the world. Its use of insinuations and its omission of vital facts is typical.

The advertisement stated that South Africa was expelled from the Olympics "at the insistence of some nations who claimed that equal opportunity in sport for the different races did not exist in South Africa". It went on to state that "Responsible voices in the Olympic movement objected to this irrational ouster but were soon drowned," and it concluded by asking "why shouldn't South Africa be re-admitted to the Olympics?"

In fact, South Africa was first excluded from the Olympics in 1964, when its team was as usual all-white because all non-whites were barred from even competing in the trials. The suggestion that this "ouster" was irrational, and that "there is no reason" why South Africa should not now take part in and even host the Olympics, can fruitfully be compared both with the fact of the original all-white teams, and events since.

After a few non-whites were included in the South African team for the 1968 Olympics, South Africa was re-admitted.

Yet not only were the members of South Africa's mixed team forbidden by the prime minister himself to compete against each other inside, or outside South Africa (where South Africa's laws do not of course apply), but the South African newspaper *Die Transvaler*, quoting government opinion, claimed that mixed sport would still not be allowed within white South Africa and that "In this sense, we are re-admitted to the Games on our own conditions". Such boasts played their part in an early re-application of the Olympics ban, for the whites' "conditions" were clearly still anti-black.

After this re-admission and then further exclusion, South Africa held its own "mini-Olympics" in Bloemfontein in March/April 1969 : the "South African Games". Black South Africans were excluded from competing, and at first it was intended that all the spectators would be white, as well. But protests from overseas eventually allowed about 750 non-white spectators to be admitted, compared with 60,000 whites.

The above contrast between the South African government's claims and the facts reveals a quite common aspect of much of this propaganda in defence of apartheid : those nations which properly objected under the Olympic Charter to the proven fact of anti-black racism in South African sport were publicly tarred as both irresponsible and irrational by an international South African advertising campaign based on innuendo and half-truths. Yet such nations were properly obeying the Olympic Charter, which forbids racism in sport.

The situation since then continues to show extensive gaps between South African fact and South African racial propaganda. In the very year in which the above advertisement was stating that there was "no reason" for continued exclusion of South Africa under the Olympic Games' anti-racial laws, it was revealed that only 331 black South Africans, but 6,393 white South Africans, were allowed to represent South Africa in international sport; i.e., in view of the disparity between the races in South Africa (72 per cent black, 17 per cent white), this represents a racial discrimination against the blacks of 80 to 1, much too great to be accounted for by arguments about alleged black dislike of various sports (for on the contrary, blacks are quite as enthusiastic as whites about sport in South Africa).

Similar flaws were apparent—although few overseas sports commentators seemed aware of them—in the early 1970s effort by the South African government to re-define South African sports as "multi-national", following the relatively new argument that each group in South Africa belongs to a "different nation", so that South Africa is really "multi-national rather than multi-racial". But since the "nation" that each South African thus belongs to is still defined, not by where he was born, but by his race as officially decided by the white-controlled South African Race Classification Board in Pretoria, the entire "multi-national" concept is revealed as nothing but apartheid under a deceptive new name.

In 1976, South Africa was claiming even more strongly that there was no racism in South African sport, and was pointing to a "new sports policy" as proof. Yet in October of that year, when several white rugby players played in a multi-racial match in Port Elizabeth on the tenth of that month, the (white) South African Rugby Board itself threatened them with suspension and said that their action "reflected badly on the country".[11] Twelve days later, the true nature of the new and allegedly non-racial sport policy was revealed in a letter from the government's Department of Sport to the Crescent Cricket Club in Vrededorp.

The department's letter referred to a statement the previous month by the prime minister himself, quoting the relevant racial section: "That the sportsmen and sportswomen of the Whites, Coloureds, Indians and Black peoples belong to their own clubs and control, arrange and manage their own sports matters." The next paragraph made clear that this total apartheid, or "apartness", in internal sport in South Africa was the much-publicized "new" sports policy.

Black sportsmen in South Africa have long suggested that the only consistent thing about their country's racial sport situation is that the government's claims, and the facts, never coincide. Be that as it may, in 1978 the gap between fact and promise apparently still existed. On the very day of an announcement by the Minister for Sport that was taken to mean the "virtual end" of compulsory apartheid in sport, South African police broke up a multi-racial soccer match and threatened the players with prosecution.[12] And soon after that the government barred white spectators from attending a multi-racial football match in Soweto because of "lack of racially segregated facilities".[13]

In May 1978 a small group of South African cricketers began a visit to Britain, New Zealand and several other countries, amid much publicity, and according to press reports at the time pledged that all aspects of South African cricket were now free of racism, claiming that there was now no excuse for other nations not to play cricket with South Africa. The very next month South Africa's most powerful local government, the Transvaal Provincial Council, re-affirmed that no mixed-race sports, including cricket, would be allowed in any Transvaal schools. The council leader said that to force integrated sport on a white child was "indoctrination".

Few overseas sportsmen have made a greater effort to be fair to white South Africa and its racial sports policies than Mr Arthur Ashe, the black American tennis player. Originally publicly critical of apartheid, he later accepted invitations to coach young black tennis players in Soweto and other black segregated townships. Before long the South African government was using photographs of Mr Ashe in its publicity material, often with the tacit suggestion that if a former critic of apartheid was prepared to "work within the system", then that system could not after all be racist.

But in 1978 Mr Ashe expressed his carefully reasoned conclusions in the *Washington Post*. "Until recently," he wrote, "I . . . thought that sport could be used to pave the way for social change and equality of opportunity in South Africa. It has not worked that way. There are those who believe that the reforms and progress made in sport are significant, but I have come to the conclusion that they are nothing more than cosmetic."[14]

There are still some all-white South African teams able to find matches and tours offered them in other white countries. Their hosts usually defend such invitations by saying that they are "building bridges of understanding with South Africa"— although it has been pointed out for years now, that such bridges are usually labelled "whites only" at both ends. The point has also been made that those who are willing to play all-white South African teams from which blacks have been racially excluded, would, to be consistent, have to be willing to play German teams from which Jews have been racially excluded, or all-black Angolan teams from which whites have been racially excluded. There appears to be considerable confusion still in the minds of many sportsmen about the irreconcilable differences between true sport ("may the best man win") and apartheid sport ("may the white man win").

Certainly on the visible, public level there has been some change in some sports in South Africa. But the continued existence of entrenched and nationwide anti-black racism in sport is a reality which the majority of South Africans—the black ones—can attest to every day. For it does seem that only in those sections of sport visible to the outside world is the new alleged "multi-racialism" applied. In a whole unreported sector of South African sport—the sports teams of various companies, including some British companies—white supremacism still tends to reign supreme. Although many such teams provide the testing-grounds of tomorrow's South African champions, most are still "whites-only". And within South Africa, such facts are not even a secret. A recent issue of a well-known South African magazine carried a photograph, for example, of a major industrial company's rugby team. Although there are more blacks in the company than whites, every one of the company's rugby team is white.

To some degree, this illustrates another factor about sport—and many other human activities—in South Africa which the West chooses to ignore. For instance, one could take the case of two typical South Africans who are identical in every respect, including physique, sporting talent, IQ and even birthplace. If both are white, then both will obviously occupy much the same level in South African sport, whether their chosen sport be rugby, cricket, surfing or tennis. But if one of them is black, then even if South Africa—as it claims to have done—removes all the purely sporting barriers to advancement, the crippling effect of the overall apartheid policy is quickly apparent.

The average white, for instance, can afford a balanced diet. The average black cannot. The white probably had good sporting facilities at school. The black probably had none. Even in the better-paid areas of commerce and industry, the white will almost certainly earn—purely because of his white skin—at least four times what the black earns, assuming both are ambitious and each is striving for advancement. So the white can afford better sporting equipment and better coaching.

Similarly, the white (in Johannesburg, for instance) will get home during daylight in summer and can train on weekdays.

The black will get home to Soweto after dark. The white will travel, perhaps overseas. The black can rarely do so, because of white-made laws and lack of money. In many cases (swimming or tennis) the white may well have his own pool or court. The black will not. At weekends, the white will belong to a sumptuously equipped white sports club (tended by blacks). The black's sporting facilities will be primitive by comparison. And so on.

Yet both these men are South Africans, born in South Africa (perhaps even in the same suburb) and distinguishable only by their different race. Proof enough that in South African sport, as in every other field of human endeavour in that country, the anti-black policy of apartheid dominates all other factors, regardless of what the white minority's propaganda might pretend. A fact which places a most interesting dilemma at the door of—for instance—the International Olympics Committee. For quite clearly, white South Africa can genuinely abolish all racial discrimination in sport as such, but the very anti-black structure of South African society itself ensures that although the blacks are in the majority, the whites have all the unsporting advantages and will doubtless continue to unfairly dominate in sport, simply by "nobbling" the black competition from birth, through laws made solely by whites.

CHAPTER SIX

Allies or Enemies of the Free World?

SOUTH AFRICA'S AFRIKANER Nationalist govern-
ment has for many years based a large part of its propaganda
and lobbying for Western military support on the claim that
South Africa has been "a reliable ally of the West in two world
wars" and is thus "unreservedly committed to the cause of the
West". There is a good deal of evidence that such claims have
been accepted at face value even in the corridors of power in
Washington, and certainly during a British parliamentary debate
recently about the arms embargo against South Africa, suggestions by Labour Party MPs that South Africa's present rulers
in reality tried to stab the West in the back in World War II
were greeted by a chorus of "Humbug!" from Conservative
Party MPs. Today, it is fashionable to sweep the generally
unique war records of South Africa's rulers under the carpet,
and to suggest that, at most, they merely "disagreed with their
country's war effort".

Those war records do, however, have considerable relevance
today, because they not only pinpoint yet another area where
shrewd South African propaganda and lobbying have shielded
the West's eyes from some quite important facts of recent
history, but there are some aspects of them which are germane
not only to the degree to which the West can trust South Africa's
ruling political party, but also to the nature of apartheid itself
and the degree to which the South African state can expect
obedience and loyalty from the black majority within its borders.
The latter being a factor crucial not only to South Africa's
stability, but to the safety of overseas investments there.

There are several pointers to the true nature of the war
record of the ruling régime in South Africa. One of the most
obvious—yet quite unnoticed—is that although white South
Africa had one of the highest enlistment rates in World War II
of any Allied country, only two or three of the Afrikaner
Nationalist government's hundreds of MPs and cabinet ministers

since 1948 ever served their country in any war, in marked contrast to the post-war governments of other Allied states. Another fact is that South African citizens who show too much interest in their present rulers' war records are likely to be banned and silenced without trial, while citizens of other countries researching these facts in South Africa have been instantly deported. To quote an ex-member of South Africa's loyal wartime military intelligence service : "Those who rule South Africa act as if they are sorry the Allies won the war".

The truth is that large numbers of Afrikaner Nationalists, including many now in the highest policy-making positions in government, the police, the administration and the armed services, did involve themselves in anti-Allied and/or pro-Nazi subversion during World War II, and did take direct action in the hope of toppling their pro-Allied wartime government so as to seize power by treachery and subversion, even if this meant the defeat of the free world and the triumph of Adolf Hitler.

The detailed story of this nation-wide high treason is available in a variety of sources, including the well-documented *White Laager* by Prof. W. H. Vatcher, *The Rise of the South African Reich* by Brian Bunting (see Bibliography), the South African press of the period—see the files in the British Museum Newspaper Library at Colindale, London—and of course the British press itself, during the war. Because of this, only the salient points will be touched on here, but some background is necessary in order to understand how black South Africans view their present predicament, in view of the war records of so many of their masters.

The wholly-Afrikaner political parties which today make up the ruling party in South Africa were, in 1939, opposed to South Africa entering the war on the Allies' side. However, in an open vote in parliament, a clear majority was obtained in mid-September 1939 for South Africa's entry as one of the Allied nations, and this decision was later vindicated when large numbers of young Afrikaners—at least as many as South Africans of British stock—volunteered to fight against Hitler.

Despite this evidence of overwhelming support for the Allied cause, the Afrikaner Nationalists (as they will hereafter be generally referred to) remained implacably opposed to the cause of the free world and, failing to persuade their government to withdraw from the war, set about to topple the government, sabotage the South African and Allied war effort and even open all South African ports and airfields to the forces of Nazi Germany and fascist Italy, by means of organized subversion.

Coupled with such aims was—and in fact had been for some time—a good deal of anti-semitic behaviour, culminating before the war in a march on parliament to stop Jewish immigration into South Africa, during which Mr Vorster's predecessor as prime minister, Dr H. F. Verwoerd—the "architect of apartheid"—claimed that "any further admission of Jews into South Africa will lead to the defiling of our white race".

As the war developed, the Afrikaner press in South Africa made it quite clear which side the more political Afrikaners supported by cheering Nazi victories, but often relegating news of Allied victories to a few lines on an inside page. So serious did the anti-Allied bias become that on 13 July 1943, Justice Millin of the South African Supreme Court delivered a judgment on Dr Verwoerd, then editor of the influential Afrikaner newspaper *Die Transvaler,* in these words : "He did support Nazi propaganda, he did make his paper a tool of the Nazis in South Africa, and he knew it."

While the mixed British/Afrikaner United Party government under General Smuts concentrated on forging South Africa into a useful weapon against the Nazi war machine, the exclusively Afrikaner parties in opposition ranged from the passively anti-Allied to the overtly pro-Nazi. Indeed the opposition leader, Dr D. F. Malan (first prime minister of the current régime), on the release of Nazi war documents many years later was found to have been negotiating with Nazi Germany behind his government's back during the first year of the war.

Of the many subversive Afrikaner organizations, two are perhaps relevant to present-day South Africa. One was the powerful, furtive Afrikaner Broederbond (Brotherhood), to which most members of the present South African government belong. The other was the often actively pro-Nazi Afrikaner Ossewabrandwag (Ox-wagon Sentinels), of which Mr B. J. Vorster, the current President of South Africa, and many of his senior colleagues of today were members or leaders. In fact, three of the four presidents of the modern South African state have war records which say a good deal about the true political attitudes of the white nation which has accepted them as heads of state.

The first president of the current South African Republic, C. R. Swart, was one of the most senior members of the Ossewabrandwag, occupying a position on its Grand Council. The third, Dr Nicolaas Diederichs, is mentioned on several pages of an important South African Military Intelligence Report into wartime Afrikaner subversion, delivered to Prime Minister Smuts on 29 March 1944. It specifically names Dr Diederichs as a Nazi "Quisling" trained in pre-war Germany at one of Adolf Hitler's indoctrination centres. The fourth president, Mr Vorster, a commandant in the Ossewabrandwag, declared at an Afrikaner *Strydag* (political rally) in 1942, "We stand for Christian Nationalism, which is an ally of Nazism."[1]

As for what many of today's leading Afrikaner Nationalists were actually doing during World War II, the London *Times* gives a clear précis. In little more than eighteen months, at a crucial stage of the war for the free world, Afrikaner Nationalists belonging to various anti-Allied groups were responsible for the following. (The dates are those of the reports.)

As a result of a mass attack on loyal South African soldiers in Johannesburg the preceding month, including the murder of one, on 5 February 1941 the South African government was forced to bring in laws providing for imprisonment for the increasingly common crime of assaulting members of the armed forces in uniform, and the spreading of subversive statements was also prohibited. The *Times* commented that there was "evidence again and again of the Ossewabrandwag's Nazi sympathies and subversive activities", and that this organization was "of precisely the same character as those which brought Adolf Hitler to power. Its methods come straight from Germany and its purpose is to introduce into South Africa by underground means the system that has flourished in Germany". Later evidence offered confirmation of this.

On 22 February an Afrikaner now active as a government-approved propagandist for apartheid was sentenced to three years imprisonment under the Official Secrets Act for illegally obtaining information about South Africa's main naval base at Simonstown. Towards the end of 1941, on 29 October, swastika armbands were found with a cache of illegal Ossewabrandwag uniforms, and on 16 December two Afrikaner saboteurs were killed by their own bomb while trying to wreck the main railway line east of Johannesburg.

On 14 January 1942 Dr D. F. Malan stated that "South Africa's participation in the war is an affront to the Afrikaner people". On 23 January 1942, a group of white South African policemen was arrested, and found to be operating a bomb factory for attacks on their own country. (In 1941 alone, 400 Afrikaner policemen were arrested for treachery, most being found to be members of the Ossewabrandwag Stormjaers.²) On 30 January, twelve power lines were blown up, in an "organized attempt to shut the mines and endanger the lives of those working underground". A long series of bomb outrages followed.

These included an attempt to dynamite police headquarters in Pretoria (4 February). Incendiary bombs placed in shops in Pretoria and telegraph wires cut in the Northern Transvaal (12 February). A statement by the leader of the Ossewabrandwag claimed that "Nazism as a world policy is perhaps the greatest turning point in one thousand years of world history", leading to a pro-Allied South African comment that "the Ossewabrandwag is blatantly pro-Nazi and explosively anti-British", and that such Afrikaner Nationalists were "Quislings".

By 12 March 1942 Prime Minister Smuts of South Africa was having to publicly rebuke the Afrikaner Nationalists for their "deplorable attacks on the Allied powers, including the USA". They replied a week later by publishing a manifesto stating that loyal non-white South Africans should not be armed even if the Japanese were on the verge of invading South Africa, as it was wrong to arm non-whites.

On 8 April there were further bomb explosions. On 22 May two post offices and a telephone exchange in the Transvaal were bombed—one of the post-office bombs killing an innocent passer-by. Three days later further time-bomb explosions destroyed telecommunications links in South Africa, and water-supply installations were dynamited. On 10 July the death sentence was passed on two Afrikaner Nationalists, Visser and van Blerk, found guilty of planting the post-office bomb that killed the passer-by. Leading Afrikaner Nationalists—including many controlling South Africa today—immediately launched a strong campaign which successfully commuted the sentence to life imprisonment (both men were released unconditionally six years later, immediately the present régime came to power in 1948).

And on 7 September 1942, an Afrikaner Nationalist was sentenced to twelve years imprisonment for trying to give the Nazi consulate in neighbouring Mozambique details of a seventeen-ship Allied convoy leaving Cape Town for the Far East, so that U-boats could intercept it and sink it.

Much of this treachery and sabotage was the work of the Ossewabrandwag. In fact, the Ossewabrandwag's own assessment of its activities and aims is on record in the shape of its leader's autobiography. Dr J. F. van Rensburg's *Their Paths Crossed Mine* (CNA, Johannesburg, 1956) makes it quite plain that a prime aim of the organization was to harm the Allied war effort by keeping large bodies of South African troops, needed in the campaign against Rommel, occupied instead in South Africa guarding strategic installations against the subversive attacks of the Ossewabrandwag, at a crucial phase in the war—1941-1942—when just such a weakening of Allied front-line man-power could have tipped the scales irrevocably in favour of Nazi Germany. "There is no doubt that the Ossewabrandwag seriously hampered the government's war effort," wrote van Rensburg, adding: "We often broke the law—and broke it shatteringly".

Such remarks are entirely consistent with statements made during World War II by various South African leaders of today. Mr B. Schoeman, for instance, a post-war cabinet minister and in the late 1960s the prime minister's right-hand man, stated on 5 November 1940 in Bloemfontein: "The whole future of Afrikanerdom is dependent on a German victory. We may as well say that openly because it is a fact. If Germany wins the war we shall be able to negotiate with her and in that way ensure the establishment of an independent republic in South Africa."[3] South Africa had at the time been at war with Germany for fourteen months.

Mr Vorster himself was even more blunt. To his comments pledging himself to support nazism, he added at that Afrikaner Nationalist anti-Allied political rally in 1942: "You can call this anti-democratic principle dictatorship if you wish."[4] On 23 September 1942, he was arrested and interned as a threat to the free world's wartime security. Also interned for similar reasons were hundreds of the Afrikaner Nationalists who now control every facet of South Africa's political and racial life.

Some pages have been devoted to the subject of the wartime treachery of Afrikaner nationalism here, because even if one

accepts the claim of some of these wartime fifth columnists to
be completely reformed today, the fact still remains that determined attempts have long been made to hide the truth from
the outside world, and even to pretend that the ruling régime
had a strictly honorable war record—judging from the self-
righteous attitude adopted by the government today.

Particularly when attacking America, South Africa's leaders
appear to be using this self-righteousness—often to good effect
amongst hard-line American conservatives—to denigrate the
American government and call into doubt its motives, its integrity and even its willingness to face up to communism; with
the ever-present innuendo that therefore the US government
has no right even to criticize South Africa in any way.

Because so few Americans are actually aware of the true war
records of many of South Africa's present leaders, the result
has been an extraordinary situation in which a South African
régime with a background of pro-Nazi wartime treachery has
been accusing America of "betraying" South Africa in its 1975
invasion of black Angola, and even to claim of that event that
"America recklessly left South Africa in the lurch"—to quote
from an angry attack on America by the South African Foreign
Minister on 18 April 1978. The degree to which South Africa
thus today resorts to bluff is perhaps a measure of its confidence
that its anti-Allied war record has by now been satisfactorily
forgotten.

But the effects of that war record persist, and may well be
governing South Africa's present, and undermining its future.
For instance, Mr Vorster's 1942 statement that he and his colleagues stood for Christian Nationalism, an ally of nazism,
referred to the type of internal society which would be set up
in South Africa in a future Afrikaner-run republic. That
republic has now existed since 1961, and its internal policy is
actually called "Christian Nationalism". Are there any important aspects of the way in which it is run which are not merely
abhorrent to the free world today, but which are in fact allied
to nazism?

The most direct and undeniable link between the South
Africa of today and the Third Reich of Nazi Germany lies in
the racial laws of the two states.

The basic race laws of South Africa are those which prevent
the "non-white" races from interbreeding with the whites; those

which inhibit the non-white races from employing or giving orders to whites; and those which deprive the non-white races of citizenship and of political and most civil rights in the land in which nearly all of them were born.

Whether these central race laws of South African apartheid are derived directly from the anti-semitic race laws of Nazi Germany is a question answered simply by comparing them.

Thus, the South African Prohibition of Mixed Marriages Act, No. 55 of 1949, forbids intermarriage between whites and non-whites and provides that any such mixed marriages contracted outside South Africa are null and void. Section 1 of the anti-semitic Nazi Nuremberg Laws ("Laws for the protection of German blood and German honour," Nuremberg, 15 September 1935) states: "Marriages between Jews and citizens of German or kindred blood are forbidden. Marriages concluded in defiance of this law are void, even if, for the purpose of evading this law, they were concluded abroad."[5] Except for the victim races, the two laws are clearly identical.

The South African Immorality Act, No. 21 of 1950, forbids sexual relations of any kind—even hand-holding or kissing—between whites and non-whites. Section 2 of the Nazi Nuremberg Laws reads: "Sexual relations between Jews and Nationals of German or kindred blood are forbidden." (It is perhaps of interest that the above two South African sex laws were introduced only some five years after their originals lapsed in Germany with the defeat of the Nazi régime.)

The South African Industrial Conciliation Act, as noted earlier, contains a clause, Section 77, which in effect denies the right of non-whites to employ whites in South Africa. Section 3 of the Nazi Nuremberg Laws is less strict, and merely enjoins that "Jews are not permitted to employ female citizens of German or kindred blood as domestic servants".

On 7 February 1978 the South African government confirmed that its Bantu Homelands Citizenship Act No. 26 of 1970, with its associated legislation, would definitely be used to deprive all black South Africans of their South African citizenship—a process now in full flood—and that this included the permanent denial of voting rights to blacks, and also denied them the right to occupy public office. The Nazi "Reich Citizenship Law" of 14 November 1935, states in article 2: "A citizen of the Reich can be that subject only who is of German or kindred blood. Only the citizen of the Reich enjoys full political rights." And in article 4: "A Jew cannot be a citizen of the Reich. He has no right to vote in political affairs and cannot occupy public office." Again, South African and Nazi race laws are seen to be essentially identical.

Possibly the next thing to come to mind is the autocratic political structure of the entire South African state, with its strong *herrenvolk* flavour. Almost all VIPs, from the state president down—including the heads of the police, post office, education, broadcasting services, foreign affairs and information department is an Afrikaner Nationalist. In many such government departments—particularly the armed forces and broadcasting—there was in the 1950s and 1960s an actual purge of many experienced men who were replaced by often inexperienced Afrikaner Nationalists. Even in South Africa's legal profession there is today still a good deal of bitterness over the way in which many sound judicial minds have been passed over so that politically "correct" Afrikaner Nationalists could be appointed as judges. And the political nature of the police was fully apparent as long ago as 1962, when in the middle of Johannesburg, police in civilian clothes attacked elderly white women holding anti-apartheid placards while the uniformed police looked on and refused to protect them. (By 1978, it had been estimated that of no less than 1,600 criminal acts of injury and damage against anti-apartheid people in South Africa, only two culprits had ever been brought to court by the South African police and convictions obtained.)

It is true, however, that such methods and attitudes, although generally frowned on by civilized states, are neither especially rare nor particularly Nazi in nature. But there are nevertheless other aspects of South African internal policy today which do seem closer to Nazi practice.

One of the most interesting is the system of forced labour implemented under the Coloured Cadets Act of 1967. This Act provides for the compulsory registration of all Coloured youths between the ages of 18 and 24. The youths can then be sent to compulsory labour "training" camps run by whites with rigid discipline. The true nature and purpose of these camps was admitted by the Afrikaner colonel in charge of one of them in 1976. They are "intended to provide the private sector with trained and disciplined workers," he said.[6] That is, they provide

cheap trained Coloured labour for white businesses in South
Africa. Workers whose employers find their work unsatisfactory
are returned to the camps for disciplining, while failure to report
in the first place when called up can result in a three-year
prison sentence. A humanitarian group which investigated this
Coloured forced-labour system noted in its report that this was
but one of many such systems "reducing significant proportions
of the South African population to unfree labour". Such systems
do not apply to white youths.

It can also quite legitimately be argued that the recent South
African "puppet" system of allowing black ghettos such as
Soweto eventually to be internally controlled by government-
approved black civic councils, is substantially identical to the
Nazi plan for classing Jewish ghettos in Germany originally,
at any rate, as "autonomous Jewish territories"; and indeed
that the overall "black homelands" policy, under which the
"racially pure" white minority forces the blacks to move "back
to" areas most of them have never set eyes on before (there to
have to register for work permits to be allowed back into
"white" South Africa) is a system largely identical to the whole
forced-labour structure of Nazi Germany as applied to "inferior" races.

This whole area of comparison between modern South Africa
and Hitler's Germany is one which consistently turns up the
most remarkable similarities. Just as "aliens" in Nazi Germany
were forbidden to remain idle, being pressed into menial service
for the Reich, so in South Africa in 1978 legislation was prepared to deal with "Idle Bantu"—any black unemployed for
any four months in any calendar year. Whites can retire whenever they wish, or not work at all. Black South Africans
attempting this—even if they could afford it—are arrested and
detained at "rehabilitation centres" or given prescribed labour
tasks at "farm colonies".

Germany's notorious Hitler Youth has a modern Afrikaners-
only echo in South Africa (or had—its official links with the
South African police now shield it from the public eye, under
the State Security Act). Formed in 1958 by a magazine of the
Afrikaner Nationalist Party's publishing house in the Transvaal,
the *Patrys* Speurklub, although not indulging in all the excesses
of the Hitler Youth, nevertheless had the constitutional right
to hunt down and arrest blacks, its twelve to eighteen-year-old

members often being monetarily rewarded for such activities by the South African police. Inevitably, this junior white police force has greatly increased black determination to be rid of white rule, yet mention of the Speurklub is absent from the West's newspapers and television alike.

There are even strong similarities between the arguments used to defend Nazi anti-semitism, and apartheid. The journalist/diplomat Bruce Lockhart recorded in *Guns or Butter* (Putman, 1938) after an extended journey through Europe, comments from Nazi apologists such as "The British have no Jewish question in the sense that Germany has. When Britain has a Jewish problem, Britain's attitude will be different." ("South Africa has a unique racial situation, and solutions suggested by other countries do not apply," is one of the favourite tenets of white South African propagandists.)

"Which do you think is preferable : a press that is controlled so that it may publish only verified news, or a press that is allowed to publish deliberate untruths?" asked a Nazi editor in *Guns or Butter*—thus neatly pre-empting the South African government's excuses for closing down Mr Percy Qoboza's black *World* newspaper in Johannesburg 40 years later.

British apologists for Nazi Germany in the 1930s, and for the white minority régimes of southern Africa in the 1970s, similarly appear to be using exactly the same questionable arguments. Conservative sources in Britain are fond of defending South Africa by claiming that black-ruled states in Africa are incompetent and corrupt. Bruce Lockhart wrote in 1937 that "powerful influences in Britain . . . were conducting a shameful propaganda describing Czechoslovakia as a ramshackle state unfit to govern itself". And the same book records that British conservative opinion was against a war with Nazi Germany "because the Germans are our blood brothers". Forty years later the Rhodesian disaster was largely due to similar conservative opinion firmly siding with the white Rhodesian minority "because they are our kith and kin".

The racial propaganda of modern South Africa and Nazi Germany shows a family resemblance, too. Of the impressions of the average foreign visitor to South Africa who has "come to see for himself", one could quote : "Somehow, all they saw, heard and experienced did not fit in with the picture of a land of oppression and persecution such as the foreign press reports had led them to expect." It is a statement typical of those one reads in South African propaganda, and indeed in the British press about white visitors to South Africa. In fact, this is taken from the very first page of the Nazi propaganda book *Look to Germany*, written by an American citizen and published in 1937 by Heinrich Hoffman, Hitler's personal photographer, in Berlin.

This 240-page, copiously illustrated book contains precisely the same rhetorical and racial arguments that have for years been a feature of white South African racial propaganda. It demands international support for nazism because it is fighting the "fist of unbounded communism", and claims that Nazi Germany is proceeding "quietly and peacefully in the manner of national-socialising, based upon recent development and the foundation of national and Christian tradition"—a sentence in which one need only replace "national-socialising" with "separate development" to turn it into South African propaganda.

Like South Africa today, Nazi propaganda of the 1930s stressed the "deeply religious" nature of the state and its leaders, warned of the dangers of "liberalistic freedom", claimed that the régime "extends a friendly hand to its neighbours", and directly parallels current South African diversionary attacks on race problems in Western countries with a paragraph attacking American treatment of negroes, and the comment "How much more considerate is Germany's treatment of her half million Jews! . . . no comparison is possible with the plight of the negro in the southern states of America"—an unconscious truth not untypical of much South African racial propaganda.

How Nazi Germany really treated the Jews, and how modern South Africa really treats blacks, is a subject which begs more extensive research, from the similarity of "Aryans only" beaches in Germany and "whites only" beaches in South Africa, to the whole basic concept of small, overcrowded "homelands" for black South Africans, and their possible ideological origins in the Nazi concept of a Jewish "homeland" in conquered Poland, from which Jews could be drawn as required to serve the "Aryan" German state. But in Germany, the racial psychosis got out of hand. (Might history repeat itself?)

In view of such facts, it is not surprising that the Afrikaner Nationalist government of South Africa is anxious to hide the war records of so many of its senior members and racial policy-makers. But the West is also largely ignorant of the fact that what has also been hidden is the *pro-Allied* war records of many black South Africans, today amongst the victims of apartheid. Some 125,000 non-white South Africans, although forbidden to bear arms, served the Allied war effort, many in the fight against Rommel. Their casualty rate was similar to that of the whites.[7] Today they are ignored.

There is, perhaps, another reason why the often pro-Nazi war records of those who rule South Africa have been so carefully camouflaged, and that is South Africa's partial dependence on modern Israel. For one wonders if Israel would be quite so friendly if the facts were better known, bearing in mind that as recently as 1971, Israeli Ambassador Mordecai Kidron said at the UN, "It is self-evident that the Jewish experience throughout the ages leads us inevitably to condemn any manifestation of racial discrimination based on colour, such as apartheid."

Despite events such as Afrikaner Nationalist collusion, in April 1945, in a campaign claiming that the Nazi extermination of the Jews was a British and American hoax to discredit Germany, between 1972 and 1977 Israel-South African trade rose more than 400 per cent,[8] and in 1977 the Israeli government, like so many others, stated that although it opposed apartheid, South Africa's internal policies were "her own affair".

However, the reason for mentioning the above points is not to get involved in any pro- or anti-Israel discussion, but simply to point out the pitfalls which can appear in the path of any nation which tends to take South African propaganda seriously. For there is little doubt, judging alone from the large number of recent and often ill-informed letters defending South Africa's race policies in the American press in particular, yet posted in Tel Aviv and Jerusalem, that an extensive South African propaganda drive has been taking place in Israel following Mr Vorster's visit there in 1975.

The pitfall is obvious. Israel's enemies are already beginning to make use of the facts that South Africa has not mentioned in its propaganda, so that today Israel is in the position of publicly and privately showing a friendly attitude towards South Africa and inevitably towards apartheid—while apparently unaware that the basic laws of apartheid, as noted earlier in this chapter, are direct copies of the very anti-semitic laws of Nazi Germany under which Jews were first classed as "sub-human" by the Hitler régime. Many Jews familiar with South Africa have thus warned urgently that any friendship or even trade between Israel and South Africa must directly undermine world sympathy for the Jewish people's experience in Nazi Germany, and the Jewish cause in general.

Yet Israel's case is merely the most direct example of the implications that must flow from the war records, racial policies and race laws of those who largely lead the South African régime today. For instance, plausible arguments abound for selling South Africa arms, installing the US Fleet at Simonstown and even inviting South Africa to join NATO. Many of these arguments are supported by the familiar claim—often in South African propaganda's own phraseology—that "South Africa was a loyal ally of the West in two World Wars". But none of these arguments mention the points brought out in this chapter—that the South Africans who are loyal allies of the West are today almost totally absent from South Africa's government, administration and policy-making boards, and that in their place one again and again finds men who, by their own statements and by the record of history itself, could not even be trusted by their own country when it was last at war, but had to be interned as a threat to Allied security. The only guarantee the West has that these men are now loyal to the West is their own statements that they are. Is this a strong-enough peg on which to hang perhaps a vital part of the security cordon of the West? The question is an important one, for it is one of the most basic axioms of war that an unreliable ally is worse than no ally at all.

There is another flaw in South Africa's arguments aimed at gaining the trust of the West. Although the Afrikaner National-ist Party is firmly in power in South Africa, the country does have (whites only) elections. It is thus not impossible that a largely non-Afrikaner (although undoubtedly still quite dis-criminatory) white government could come to power in South Africa, similar to the Smuts' wartime government. If this occurred when the West was relying strongly on South Africa's help and strategic situation in a confrontation with the Communist states, is there any guarantee that the Afrikaner Nationalists would not, as they have done twice before in living memory, resort to armed subversion on behalf of the West's enemies in order to topple the new government and regain power—thus perhaps crippling the West when South Africa's help or at least stability was most needed? The suggestion may seem unfair, but it was precisely at a time when the entire free world was fighting for its life against Nazi Germany that the Afrikaner Nationalists, in the words of one of them, "seriously hampered the government's war effort. A not inconsiderable military element had to be retained in South Africa as a strategic reserve for possible emergencies" caused by Afrikaner Nationalist sabotage, subversion and high treason.

Finally, there is the internal situation. Few people outside South Africa understand that by and large, the black majority group in South Africa are fully aware of the manner in which the present ruling party attempted to gain control of that country illegally, by terrorism and by subversion, in wartime— despite the fact that the Afrikaner Nationalists, unlike black South Africans, have always had the vote.

An understanding of the attitude which such knowledge creates amongst the five-in-every-six South Africans who are not white is essential for any rational prediction of the future of that country—and it explains in some detail why today, the Afrikaner Nationalist government over-reacts with such ferocity to any action or even opinion which can by any stretch of the imagination be classed as "disloyal" or "unpatriotic". In fact, the government has recently publicly denounced as "traitors" clergymen who advise South Africans to become conscientious objectors in a future race war, and in 1977 a law was introduced making it a criminal offence to persuade anyone to so object.

The double standards which such attitudes create throughout the entire fabric of South African life and culture have been likened by some observers to those of the most cynical Latin American "banana republic", wherein each new ruling party makes illegal the very acts of treachery by which it itself gained power. And so the result is the same in each case; the ruled have none of that tacit respect for the rulers and their laws which is the sole basis of any civilized and stable society.

This is a fact about South Africa which the West seems determined to ignore. Yet the evidence of it is plain to be seen at every mass political trial of black South Africans by white South Africans. Again and again, the black attitude is less of

fear, caution or anger, than of profound contempt for the white
man and his entire legal and political system. For the blacks
know something that is rarely if ever spelled out in the white
news-services' reports on South African political trials: the
blacks know that they had no say in electing the government
which created the laws under which blacks are tried and punished. They know that they had no say either in formulating
those laws. They know that the police force is a white man's
police force, the courts are white men's courts, the prisons are
white men's prisons. They also know that by the white man's
rules of ownership, South Africa belongs to the black man by
right of prior settlement, but the white man holds it by force
of arms. And above all, they know that the entire system of
laws under which "subversive" blacks are arrested, detained,
tried, convicted and punished was created by a white régime
which itself, when it happened to suit it, in the words of the
South African President's own wartime superior "often broke
the law, and broke it shatteringly".

The black South African therefore tends to view the entire
white racial, political and legal structure of his country with a
vast derision. He owes neither duties nor responsibilities towards
such a system, and he knows it.

In fact, it is a bitter joke amongst many black South Africans
that if they were merely to voice the type of statements made
by white South Africa's present leaders during World War II,
they would without doubt disappear into unlimited detention
under the South African Terrorism Act. The point is easily
illustrated simply by bringing such statements up to date. If a
black South African were to echo Mr Vorster's famous 1942
statement today it would come out as "We stand for black
nationalism, which is an ally of communism. You can call this
anti-democratic principle dictatorship if you wish."

As noted earlier in this chapter, one of Mr Vorster's closest
colleagues, B. Schoeman, said publicly on 5 November 1940,
"The whole future of our Afrikaner people is dependent on a
German victory. If Germany wins, we will be able to negotiate
with her." Today's black version of that would be: "The whole
future of us blacks depends on a Russian victory. If Russia wins,
we will be able to negotiate with her." And one can imagine
what would happen today to a black South African who said
"Communism as a world policy is perhaps the greatest turning

point in 1,000 years of human history." Yet with one word
(nazism) altered, that is exactly what Mr Vorster's superior in
the Ossewabrandwag, Dr Hans van Rensburg, said in 1942.

It has often been said in criticism of the white régime in
Pretoria that when black South Africans do not resist their
oppression with acts of violence, the régime says that this
proves that the blacks "accept apartheid". And that when the
blacks do react with violence, the régime then says that this
proves that the blacks are "incurably violent" and must therefore be controlled by force.

This criticism is certainly true, and there are many examples
of such "heads I win, tails you lose" sophistries to be found in
white South Africa. A much more urgent truth, however, is
the fact that because of the examples of violence and treason
set by so many of South Africa's present rulers when their
country was last at war, today's five-in-six South African non-
white majority is fully aware that it is bound by no moral
prohibitions on the use of identical tactics—armed terrorism,
sabotage, bomb outrages and even murder—in order to similarly
wrest control of their country by force. This sheds an often
unsuspected light on the true state not only of South Africa's
security, but also of the safety of overseas investments, and of
future internal order in South Africa. The whites have set the
precedent for armed revolution. The blacks may well follow that
precedent at any time. Yet the West has for years been kept in
ignorance of the true nature of this psychological and racial
time-bomb under white rule, and is still making its policies for
southern Africa as if all such factors and attitudes did not exist.

Worse, the conservative viewpoint in the West—under white
South African prompting to see all resistance to apartheid as
"Communist"—is likely to view any black uprising in South
Africa through a distorting mirror, in which the oppressive
white rulers are seen as endangered democrats, while the
oppressed black majority is automatically labelled as terrorists;
a misassessment with possibly disastrous implications for black/
white relations in Africa and the world.

For from the viewpoint of black South Africa—and probably
most of Africa as well—the blacks are merely struggling for
human rights in their own country against white leaders for
whom they never voted (being forbidden to) and who have
already proved that *they* are the terrorists by setting the crucial

precedent—that of trying to bring down their own government by force in wartime.

The rights and wrongs of each side's viewpoint can be argued at length, but what is surely most relevant is that all the pre-conditions for a violent explosion—oppression, numerical strength, easy recognition of the enemy, mass anger and, as noted above, a lack of moral hindrances to action—now co-exist in South Africa. And the oppression, the numerical strength of the oppressed and their mass anger increase almost daily, while white South Africa insists that all is peaceful, criticizes the West for its doubts about South Africa's future and tries to encourage further Western investment in apartheid.

Yet there is no doubt that the West would be wise to make very sure of its facts about South Africa before listening to such encouragement. For within the ruling hierarchy of Afrikaner nationalism, even the limited and largely non-violent black resistance so far to the all-white power structure is being greeted with extravagant threats of a "counter-revolution by whites" against the blacks' alleged "unfair and unprovoked aggression".[9] And there is evidence that such dangerous over-sensitivity has deep roots within the Afrikaner culture. For 120 years ago, Dr David Livingstone himself recorded of the Transvaal Boers that even rumours of black disaffection "assume all the appearance and proportions of a regular insurrection. Severe measures then appear as imperatively called for, and, however bloody the massacre that follows, no qualms of conscience ensue : it is a dire necessity for the sake of peace."[10]

CHAPTER SEVEN

South African Interference in Other Countries

"Germany does not interfere in the internal affairs of Britain. She has a right to expect that the British should not interfere in hers."—Nazi editor-in-chief of the *Deutsche Allgemeine Zeitung*, in 1937.

"The cornerstone of our policy is the principle of non-interference in each other's domestic affairs."—The South African Minister for Information, addressing the Los Angeles World Affairs Council, 6 June 1975.

To LINK DIRECTLY the two quotations above would perhaps be rather facile, but together they do offer some link between the preceding chapter and this one. And there is certainly no doubt that the pledge of "non-interference" is one of the most-used weapons in the South African propaganda armoury.

"I want to state again, clearly, that we do not interfere in the internal affairs of other countries," said Prime Minister Vorster in his famous "Give South Africa six months" speech in 1974—just one year before he sent his armed forces into Angola to prevent a political party South Africa disliked from taking power (four years later, South Africa was still flying in arms to anti-government guerrillas within Angola). "South Africa does not prescribe to Rhodesia what sort of solution should be found. That is in accordance with our principle of non-interference in the domestic affairs of others", said South Africa's Foreign Minister in London on 22 September 1975, as South African troops pushed deeper and deeper into Angola.

There seems little doubt that this aspect of South Africa's overall campaign to manipulate world opinion rests on the hope that if the West can be persuaded that South Africa is innocent of aggressive intent, it might give help if South Africa were militarily interfered with, or even only had sanctions applied against it. A further white South African fear is one that has long haunted this minority, and especially the Afrikaners—that of the black majority in final revolt against apartheid and its creators. In the latter case, the West would inevitably have to sacrifice its own democratic principles in order to help white South Africa, for it would be siding with a small white minority against the majority of South Africans on a racial basis. Not only could this lose Africa to the West for ever, but any Communist nation which then stepped in and challenged the West might gain incalculable prestige with much of the Third World.

However, such speculations are less important at this stage than the answers to the two questions that the South African "non-interference" campaign immediately raises: 1. Might not the outside world have some kind of moral right anyway to interfere in South Africa on behalf of the great majority of that country's people—the non-whites? And 2. Is it in any case true that South Africa does not interfere in the internal affairs of other countries?

Although the first question tends to be rhetorical rather than practical, there does appear to be at least some moral justification *per se* for much of the outside criticism of South Africa's racial policies, and possibly for active interference in them as well. Foremost amongst such justifications, at least where British interference is concerned, is the largely forgotten fact that South Africans of all colours were once British subjects, but that the white South African minority took the five-in-six non-white majority out of the British Commonwealth without asking their consent or even opinion, after a "whites only" referendum in 1960. (This is roughly equivalent to the black minority in Britain or America reducing the white majorities' citizenship rights in those countries without the whites' consent.)

There are other aspects to be considered. If "South Africa" is taken to be the sum of its people, anti-apartheid activities and/or other interference might well be justifiable as interference aimed at materially helping the great majority of that country's people; i.e., morally right if legally doubtful. Similarly, the sale by the outside world of arms, or materials such as oil to the white South African minority, which restricts to itself the right to carry arms and decides on the use to which strategic materials may be put, is by strict definition both anti-South African and anti-black. The point is an interesting one because,

6—RPASA * *

having massively armed only the white side in the South African racial confrontation, unless the West now arms the black side as well it is by definition anti-black in its attitude towards the majority of the people of South Africa. (A vital point easily enough substantiated by a simple analogy : if the city of New York were to pass an ordinance allowing any non-Jew to buy a gun, but forbidding the sale of guns to New York's large number of Jews, would nations supplying guns to New York shops be anti-semitic or not?)

Such arguments may be rhetorical, but are mentioned here because they show how an increasing number of black South Africans view the situation in which they are forced to live. But the second question—does South Africa interfere in other countries?—is far from rhetorical, for the facts are those of very recent history, and involve almost every country in southern Africa. The recent known examples of physical interference are as follows :

Rhodesia

South Africa has repeatedly denied that it has interfered in Rhodesia in any way during the time that the illegal Smith government was ruling the country and Rhodesia's only legal government was the British government in London. "It must be fully understood that I do not want to interfere in any way in the internal affairs of Rhodesia," assured the South African Prime Minister in the senate on 23 October 1974.[1] On 27 July 1977 the South African Foreign Minister reminded the world that "South Africa's record in trying to bring the various parties together in Rhodesia speaks for itself", and that South Africa's rôle was "not to interfere".

But on the night of UDI itself—11 November 1965—the government-controlled South African Broadcasting Corporation was saying very much the opposite. An anonymous speaker—later identified as a past Director of Information at the South African embassy in London—stated that Rhodesia had taken its self-determination as its right—as "its European heritage". The speaker continued, "There is between Rhodesia and South Africa a kind of spiritual relationship", and warned, "It cannot, and may not be expected that South Africa will play the rôle of a passive onlooker."

On the next night, the same speaker said that "Rhodesia, and the rest of the world, knows where South Africa stands on this issue", and before the week was out the South African Broadcasting Corporation had launched a public attack on anti-UDI comment in the Rhodesian press, supporting Mr Ian Smith's gagging of that press with the introduction of stringent press censorship regulations. And in the meantime, less than three days after UDI a South African cabinet minister, farewelling a team of South African government railway engineers on their way to help Rhodesian Railways, said "South Africa's frontier is now at the Zambesi".[2] Within weeks, South African oil was being railed into Rhodesia.

The South African military involvement in Rhodesia followed less than two years later. In 1967 several hundred South African police (who receive army training and are in effect as well-armed as the South African army) were sent to Rhodesia to help keep the black population subdued. News of their presence leaked out, but South Africa denied it. In 1968, however, the South African government actually boasted that it was helping the rebel Rhodesian régime militarily, and ignored protests from Britain.

By the early 1970s, there were at least 3,000 armed South African militia in Rhodesia, assisting the illegal rebel régime and at times killing black Rhodesians. Their armaments included mortars, armoured cars, machine guns and helicopter gun-ships, some of which were left behind with the Rhodesian army when South Africa decided for political reasons to withdraw in 1975. That such armed interference in a British country on behalf of an illegal minority anti-black government was, however, considered "normal" by South Africa—despite its pledges of "non-interference"—was shown by a variety of statements within South Africa by government politicians. But perhaps one of the most significant pointers to real white South African feelings on this subject came in the February 1977 issue of the Afrikaner children's magazine *Patrys*, published by the ruling Afrikaner Nationalist Party and distributed to most white schools. A story "As Die Kat Weg is", set in the Rhodesian bush with a detachment of white South African militia, treated as entirely normal that armed and uniformed white South Africans should invade neighbouring countries and kill their black citizens. (In 1978, it was revealed that the South African army and air force was once again illegally and surreptitiously in action in Rhodesia, despite black protests.[3])

Swaziland

In 1973, two squads of armed South African political police took part in an armed palace coup on behalf of the political party most sympathetic to South Africa, following which the just-concluded election was declared null and void, the parliamentary opposition abolished and several of its leaders imprisoned without trial by the new pro-South African dictatorship.

Angola

In 1975 the South African army and air force, already stationed in strength in the UN territory of Namibia (South West Africa) in defiance of both a UN resolution and a World Court judgment defining their presence there as illegal, launched a major attack on the black country of Angola, in support of one of several groups contesting the leadership after the Portuguese colonial administration had relinquished control. The political convolutions need not be mentioned here, although what could perhaps be mentioned is something that the West's press and television services tended to play down or ignore: that for centuries the indigenous black Angolans had been the unwilling subjects of the Portuguese, that thousands had been massacred by the white police and army in the previous ten years alone, and that Angola is not even a neighbour of South Africa's—the two states at their nearest are 500 miles apart. Clearly, South Africa had no right—historical, racial or geographical—to interfere in any manner at all.

But in September 1975, as it was becoming evident that the so-called Marxist MPLA in Angola would form the government of the newly independent state, South Africa's armed forces crossed its southern border from Namibia. By mid-October, the heavily-armed South Africans were at least 200 miles inside Angola, and by mid-November—at about the time the first Cuban troops, there as a direct result of South African interference, were landing at Luanda—the South African armed forces were close to Lobito, 300 miles inside Angola and 800 miles from South Africa's nearest border.

At that point in time—on 18 November 1975—the South African Minister of Foreign Affairs made an extraordinary speech to a joint meeting of the Royal African Society and the Royal Institute of International Affairs at Chatham House in London. Referring specifically to the events of the previous twelve months, he said—and the quotation here is from the South African Department of Information's own published transcript—that "During this period we have maintained our scrupulously correct stance of *non-interference* with regard to developments in Mozambique and Angola."[4] (My italics).

(One can perhaps sympathize with an African diplomat who some weeks later remarked that South African "non-interference" in its neighbours' affairs was becoming quite as dangerous to those neighbours as was Hitler's policy of "non-aggression" towards Germany's neighbours.)

In January 1976, Mr Vorster, while continuing to claim that South Africa never interfered in its neighbours' affairs, publicly accused the free world of "shirking its duty" by not joining South Africa in invading Angola. In April 1978, the new South African Foreign Minister publicly accused America of "recklessly leaving South Africa in the lurch" during the 1975 invasion of Angola. And the very next month South Africa launched another armed strike deep into Angola, killing some 600 or so black men, women, children and babies at Cassinga.

The only evidence that these were, as South Africa claimed, all SWAPO guerrillas from Namibia were statements to that effect by the South African army. The Angolan authorities, however, invited foreign journalists and film crews to see the results of the South African raid for themselves, and these independent observers saw and filmed some 400 bodies of black women, children and babies, most of the women dressed not in uniforms, but in frocks. (The British mass media almost ignored such independent reports, preferring instead to publicize the unsubstantiated South African version.)

Namibia (South West Africa)

Here, too, South Africa has for some time been insisting that it does not interfere in others' internal affairs—despite the fact that the white minority in the UN mandate of Namibia are almost all South African citizens, and the Balkanization of Namibia into "homelands" for mainly white benefit is not only identical to the South African Bantustan policy but was created by the Odendaal Plan—Odendaal being the name of a South African administrator. However, as the Namibian situation is a complex study in itself, two sets of quotations give sufficient indication of whether or not South Africa's policy of "non-interference" applies to Namibia.

Early in 1975, the South African Prime Minister denied any South African interference at all in Namibia by stating "We are not occupying South West Africa" and "South Africa does not claim for itself an inch of South West African territory".[5]

But in *Patrys* magazine for September and October 1976—more than a year later—a series of advertisements appeared calling on young Afrikaner South Africans to join the South African civil service, police and railway police. The civil service advertisement carried a map which showed Namibia as a province of South Africa. The South African police advertisement—illustrated with a photograph of a young white man in full battle-kit—noted that applicants "bereid is om in enige afdeling van die Mag en op enige plek in die Republiek of Suidwes-Afrika te werk" ("You must be ready to serve in any part of the police force in any place in South Africa or South West Africa"), and the South African railway police—who are also armed—asked for applicants to help guard railways, ports and airports in South Africa and South West Africa.

As noted earlier, *Patrys* is published by the ruling Afrikaner Nationalist Party in South Africa. Four of the five South African prime ministers since 1948 have served as chairman of the board which publishes it. It thus reflects official policy, which appears to be the very opposite of the then prime minister's pledges.

A further contrast with South Africa's claim neither to desire any part of Namibia nor to be interfering there in any way, is provided by the South African Uranium Act, No. 37, which places all uranium mined at Rossing in Namibia under South African government control. Thus South Africa has been controlling this UN territory's strategic minerals, while the South African police control Namibia's indigenous people; this being described as "non-interference".

(Many excuses and reasons have been offered for South Africa's behaviour over Namibia, but there is in fact a remarkably exact parallel case elsewhere in the world against which South Africa's interference in this UN mandate can be precisely measured. For Namibia was not the only former German territory handed over in 1919 by the League of Nations to a member nation of the British Empire to administer. Another was Papua New Guinea, given to Australia to bring to nation-hood. Rarely have two mandate-holders acted more differently, because Australia mainly adhered to the terms of the mandate, did not pour thousands of police and troops into Papua, did not create artificial "homelands", did not exploit that territory for the exclusive benefit of its white minority, did not arrest, torture and imprison its indigenous leaders, did not use it as a jumping-off military base for the armed invasion of neigh-bouring countries, but instead, in 1976, openly brought it to full self-government without prevarication, and with the full approval of the UN teams who were always welcome to visit the territory and interview its inhabitants for themselves. The contrast between Australia's behaviour and South Africa's may thus offer a valuable insight into the true attitudes of South Africa towards its neighbouring black states and to the whole concept of human freedom.)

Lesotho
At the beginning of March 1978, it was announced that South Africa had "closed its frontiers with Lesotho, in an apparent effort to force the recognition of the so-called South African Bantustan of Transkei, and the government of Lesotho has appealed to the Common Market for help because of the food shortages created by the blockade." (*The Guardian*, London, 4 March 1978). This particular action by South Africa may well have a significance stretching both into international affairs, and far into the future; because a blockade of this kind is exactly the type of boycott and sanctions which South Africa, as part of its argument against the possible imposition of international sanctions against itself, denies ever using. South Africa has thus set the precedent for the very kind of sanctions campaign it most fears, against itself. It also clearly illustrates how South Africa is the main agency in introducing communism into southern Africa, because by June 1978, Lesotho had forged a pact with Cuba, in self-defence, as a direct result of South Africa's embargo.

CURRENT INTERFERENCE BY SOUTH AFRICA

At the time of writing, South Africa is still refusing to remove its troops and police from the UN territory of Namibia, and is increasing its armed support of more than four years' standing for guerrilla forces fighting against the internationally recognized government of Angola, mainly in the south of that sovereign state. In thus offering direct military aid to rebel forces attempting to unseat a legitimate black government in Africa, South Africa has set another precedent for future action against itself : namely, it has lost all moral right to protest if other states, including Communist ones, now militarily support a rebel force within South Africa aimed at bringing down the South African government by guerrilla warfare or even urban terrorism.

South Africa has, in fact, now opened the doors of precedence both to international sanctions and to armed interference in its own affairs.

There have been lesser cases of South African interference in other countries, but the above are sufficient against which to test the oft-repeated promise of South Africa's "scrupulously correct stance of non-interference" in the internal affairs of other countries. However, there are less physical ways in which one can interfere in the affairs of other nations. South Africa itself, for instance, angrily declared late in 1977 that mere criticism by the USA of events such as the mass bannings of individuals, organizations and newspapers in South Africa was "unwarranted interference" in South Africa's internal affairs. But does South Africa interfere in the affairs of America and the West in ways perhaps more serious than simple criticism, however strong?

Earlier chapters in this book may have shed some light on a quite important aspect of South Africa's interaction and relations with the outside world which has almost wholly escaped notice in the past. This is, simply, that much of the confusion, emotion, misunderstanding and bitter arguments—as in the UN—about South Africa derives from the very size of the gap between South African progaganda about apartheid, and the realities of apartheid. Perhaps it is going too far to say, as a disillusioned ex-official of South Africa's information services once did : "To every South African fact there is an equal and opposite government distortion", but it is certainly true that apartheid and its often very plausible propaganda rationales do create a good deal of acrimony overseas; a perhaps unsuspected case in point being the way often falsely-presented South African interests were allowed to force their way into the 1971 British Commonwealth conference to such a degree that at one stage there was a possibility that the Commonwealth might actually break up because of them. South Africa's part in Rhodesian oil-sanctions breaking is a more recent case.

The fact is, too, that by the very nature of the general disagreement between South Africa and the outside world on whether segregation or integration of the races is the better policy, racial disturbances outside South Africa not only help the case for apartheid but often feature strongly in South Africa propaganda for it. Causal links between South Africa and such racial troubles elsewhere do not seem to be directly established, but there is another aspect of some significance. This is that South African racial propaganda does encourage segregationist opinions and statements in other countries, as in the British Conservative Party's constituency group which some years ago called for "separate development of the races" in Britain, the similar call by the National Front in Australia in 1978, and a much earlier suggestion by a youth conference of Australia's ruling conservatives in the state of Victoria for "South African apartheid to be applied in Australia". All such statements materially add to inter-race hostility in the countries concerned.

One has only to read a small sample of South African racial propaganda over the years to realize that South Africa is, knowingly or unknowingly, the "propaganda factory" for white racists and segregationists the world over. The multi-million pound exercise, whose shrewd and plausible arguments carry a tacit message of white superiority and black inferiority, tends to rot the fruit on the laboriously-grown trees of racial harmony everywhere on this planet. Yet the propaganda is not only allowed to flow unchecked into country after country whose legislation forbids the very practice—segregation of the races— which the propaganda is designed to make acceptable, but many newspapers and television services appear anxious to encourage South African officials to spread their propaganda so that their audience will "get the South African side of the story". That it is almost solely the white minority side which is thus told, seems to have escaped many people's attention.

(Some of the above points raise an interesting question. In Britain, for instance, segregation of the races is forbidden by law. In Britain, also, drug-trafficking is forbidden by law. A foreign country which flooded Britain with propaganda eulogizing the benefits of drug-trafficking as a national policy would soon be called to account by the British government. Why then has no action at all been taken against a foreign country which has for years been flooding Britain with propaganda eulogizing the benefits of racial segregation as a national policy?)

If one looks at South Africa's international publicity operations from another largely ignored point of view, its capacity for creating racial stresses in other countries becomes a little more obvious. Black Britons and black Americans, for instance, often do not take kindly to advertisements in their mass media for South African holidays or jobs which partly or fully exclude black customers and applicants. Such blacks can in fact holiday in South Africa—but only after rigorous checking and a reluctant visa from the local South African consulate, and after accepting that their holiday will be far more restricted than those of whites. South African jobs, on the other hand, are strictly "whites only", although the advertisements rarely if ever say so—thus adding, from many blacks' point of view, dishonesty to anti-black racism in their own country's newspapers.

The subject is a large one, but a simple question might help white people to understand how it feels to be black in such cases. If the entire Caribbean area had a policy of *anti-white* apartheid, so that almost all good hotels, beaches, restaurants and night clubs were barred to whites, and whites were forbidden to take any good job or buy property of any kind in the Caribbean, then what would be the reaction of whites in Britain, Europe and America to glossy advertisements offering holidays, jobs and property in the Caribbean—but which never mentioned that all such things were largely or wholly barred to those with white skins—so that all whites were rebuffed when answering the advertisements?

Overall, it seems clear that the very existence of apartheid in South Africa must have some quite harmful effects on race relations elsewhere in the world, but the degree to which this occurs is probably a matter of opinion. Perhaps an analogy suggested some years ago by a South African Jew encapsulates the whole subject. "If a foreign country were for many years to operate a massive world-wide propaganda campaign with the theme that Jews should be kept segregated from Gentiles, including the tacit message that Jews are thus inferior to Gentiles, would such a campaign improve the lot of the world's Jews—or give encouragement to the forces of anti-semitism?"

Finally, there is a significant corollary to South Africa's record of political, economic and military interference in the affairs of other states in southern Africa. It lies in the theory, gaining increasing credence in many quarters, that South Africa's refusal even to quietly criticize—and indeed her full support for—the anti-black Portuguese administrations in Mozambique and Angola up to the time of the Portuguese coup in April 1974 helped materially in opening the door to communism in those vital parts of southern Africa.

The theory rests on solidly established facts. The first is that the Portuguese racial system, which gave rise to the powerful black resistance groups of FRELIMO in the east and the MPLA in the west, was considerably less liberal than the politicians and press of Portugal's Western allies pretended. The Larousse *Encyclopaedia of World Geography* noted of Mozambique in 1964: "Education, medical services and housing are almost non-existent for the Africans, and it is estimated that only three per cent of the Africans are literate. Six months' labour every year is compulsory for all African male adults. This provides plentiful cheap labour for the undercapitalized Portuguese farmers and makes it hard for Africans to develop their own cash crops. The system is rigorously enforced and produces widespread resentment." Conditions in Angola were similar.

Yet far from attempting to point out to the Portuguese the dangers of their racial policy, South Africa's overwhelming attitude was that the Portuguese were "too soft", as anyone living in South Africa at that time was made well aware of. Many white South Africans even complained that the Portuguese *assimilado* system of making some blacks "honorary whites" would lead to the collapse of white authority in southern Africa—despite the fact that after 450 years of Portuguese rule the percentage of *assimilado* blacks in Mozambique was only 0.08 per cent.

The effect of such anti-black attitudes amongst the Portuguese administration—coupled with the refusal of the West to help the black majority in any way—was to push the indigenous populations of both Mozambique and Angola straight into the arms of the Communist world, and produce the situation which exists today. South Africa's frequent and loud complaints about the "Marxist governments" in both these states should therefore be viewed, surely, in the light of South Africa's considerable culpability in bringing those Marxist governments about, as even a little understanding for the sufferings of the black populations of Mozambique and Angola might well have reduced some of the major cruelties which resulted in both states going Communist.

It might seem unnecessarily critical of white South Africa, after drawing attention to its extensive and often disruptive interference in other states in southern Africa, to even suggest that there might have been other cases in which South Africa actually should have interfered. But such comment is felt to be both pertinent and legitimate simply because South Africa has, since 1976, been trying to blame America and to a lesser extent the free world as a whole for the increasingly dangerous situation in southern Africa.

A typical example of this was the major policy speech on 8 April 1978 by the South African Foreign Minister, reported throughout the world, in which America was bluntly accused of being almost entirely to blame for any Communist threat in southern Africa, and America and Britain were jointly held to blame for any future Communist aggression in Namibia and Rhodesia. Yet as noted above, the only states in a position to snuff out the fires of the black backlashes which led to Communist rule in Angola and Mozambique were Portugal and South Africa, and the latter not only refused to help ameliorate the oppression of blacks in those countries but in fact gave both moral support and munitions to the Portuguese oppressors; while in Namibia the sole reason for the rise of an armed resistance movement favourably inclined towards Moscow was South Africa's illegal annexation of that UN territory and its application both of apartheid and the unfair Bantustan-style carving up of that territory to give most land and most mineral wealth to its small white minority.

The facts therefore strongly suggest that the major source of destabilization over a period of many years in southern Africa has been white South Africa itself.

There is, however, a chain of other facts which offers an intriguing side-light to this subject. For if one charts the allegiances of the pure-white political party which rules South Africa, one finds over the years a remarkable capacity for always choosing not merely the morally wrong side, but the losing side as well.

Thus, in World War II the Afrikaner Nationalists supported the Nazis. The Nazis lost. The Afrikaners allied themselves to the Portuguese in Mozambique and Angola. The Portuguese lost. They solidly supported Rhodesia's UDI in 1965. At time of writing, it is collapsing. In the 1960s, they swore never to give up Namibia. In the 1970s, their hold over it is uncertain. And in 1975 they backed UNITA against the MPLA in Angola —and UNITA lost.

Rarely can the governing party in any country have so consistently displayed an inability to understand which way the winds of change are really blowing. An inability which may have played some part in white South Africa's catastrophic record of interference in other countries' affairs, yet which has been repeatedly hidden from view by the very effectiveness of South Africa's own deceiving—and self-deceiving—propaganda.

And what helped hide all these things from view was undoubtedly the way in which southern African affairs have been reported by the international mass media. South Africa's interference in Swaziland and its recent trade boycott of defenceless Lesotho were almost wholly ignored by the West's television and press, which preferred to give much larger coverage to unproven guesses about the possible presence of a few Cuban troops amongst the invading rebels in Zaire in the first half of 1978. And certain sections of the British press largely ignored, for the entire eight years from 1967 to 1975, the well-documented presence of thousands of armed white South African militia illegally present and engaged in anti-black warfare on British Commonwealth soil in Rhodesia.

Similarly, despite the overwhelming importance of the subject, the mass media in the West have consistently played down often well-researched reports indicating that South Africa was building a nuclear weapon capability, culminating in the massively-documented 1978 book *The Nuclear Axis* (Friedman, London) which uses photostats of confidential official South African documents to show that South Africa, if not already a nuclear power, is very close to becoming one. And the "conspiracy of silence" around oil sanctions-breaking is well known.

Perhaps it only remains to be said that when one adds the

high probability that South Africa now has its own nuclear weapons to its aggressive armed interference, government denials in the face of the facts and a certain blindness in predicting the results of its actions, then it becomes even more urgent for the world at large to judge white South Africa's nature and true intentions not on what it has been saying, but on what it has actually been doing. Especially now that the revelations of "Muldergate" have shown what degree of reliance can be placed on some of South Africa's most earnest protestations of innocence.

CHAPTER EIGHT

South Africa and Communism

"South Africa is, and always has been, anti-Communist and unreservedly committed to the cause of the West. Her leaders have repeatedly stated that the Republic would do her duty in the event of a military confrontation between the West and communism."—*South African Quiz*, published by the South African government and distributed free in large numbers throughout the world.

IN ORDER TO establish whether or not South Africa is genuinely anti-Communist—or might even in some respects be Communist itself—it is necessary to define what one means by "Communist". And this is something that South Africa never does. Instead, that country uses the words "Communist" and "communism" in a way that at times is identical to the use by earlier generations of Europeans of words such as "Bolshevik", "heretic" and even "witch". For, as noted earlier, almost all South African descriptions of the arms and explosives used by blacks against whites in southern Africa are preceded by adjectives such as "Communist" or "Iron Curtain"—even when such terminology is semantically ridiculous.

The fact is that "Communist" has several meanings, not just one. It can be used to describe a one-party state based to greater or lesser degree on the principles of Lenin. It can be used as a kind of shorthand to encompass the various international and military schemes and gambits of Left-wing states—as in "the Communist threat to the West". Also, it describes a system whereby, hopefully, the political principles of "from each according to his ability, to each according to his needs" are in some way being applied. And finally, it can—and usually is— used simply to denote a way of life in which human rights are crushed and a despotic "leftist" minority organizes the state for its own ends. Perhaps this is the most common meaning.

Similarly, "anti-Communist" has several definitions, not all of them as creditable as many people would pretend. For Adolf Hitler was, after all, one of the most committed anti-Communists of them all.

Now that the word "Communist" has been more clearly defined, it can be seen that South Africa normally uses it as a trigger-word for the releasing of hostile emotions amongst those politically inclined to the right. So it could be worthwhile to look at what lies behind such use, by examining South Africa's true attitudes towards tyranny, as revealed in its deeds, rather than just its words.

The following short article, by this author, was originally published in 1977 by Gemini News Service. Apart from some updating and editing, it serves well enough to put a point of view which has been largely ignored by all but a minuscule fraction of the West's politicians and mass media, but which perhaps, in the West's long-term interests, needs now to be studied more closely.

> " 'We must live where the State tells us, and cannot own land here where we were born. We must rent our accommodation from the State—four tiny concrete rooms for a family, and six to a room in bleak State hostel blocks for single workers. The police can enter our homes and search for political material at any time. We are forbidden to strike, and on average one in thirty of us is arrested every year for not carrying our identity documents with us. Every year thousands of us are exiled to remote places if unemployed, or if our documents are not in order. We must have a permit to travel around our own country, and passports are usually withheld. We have no say in the government which rules us, or the laws which control us. We are prisoners in the land of our birth.'

"It sounds like a victim of communism, quoted from a Solzhenitsyn novel. It is in fact a fairly typical South African— a black South African worker living in all-black Soweto, outside white Johannesburg, and prompted to voice his complaints by years of racial oppression culminating in the police killings of black schoolchildren from 1976 onwards.

"South Africa's attempts to position itself in the eyes of the white West as a typical free-enterprise democracy, totally committed to the anti-Communist cause, reached its peak in 1975 in its armed invasion of black Angola—an act of war aimed at installing an Angolan government more to South Africa's taste than the Communist MPLA. The official South African film of the war, *Bridge 14*, gave hero-status to a white lieutenant of the South African army who after killing eleven black Angolans on their own soil boasted 'I am not fighting for South Africa, but for Jesus Christ, against the anti-Christ forces of communism.' Even South Africa has now had to admit its indefensible invasion of Angola in reality immensely strengthened Communist influence in Africa, leading directly to the abortive Kissinger mission on Rhodesia and the drawing-up of today's racial battle lines.

"South Africa has in fact been claiming for years that it is 'the West's bastion against communism in Africa'. But evidence is piling up that South Africa's definition of 'communism' is a quite extraordinary one, and some observers are already remarking that where human freedoms are concerned, the black worker born in Johannesburg is in reality less free than the Russian worker in Moscow or the Czech worker in Prague. For the Communist worker can by talent and effort get to the top in his country's government, industry, armed services, entertainment, science or the professions. The black South African cannot—all such positions in South Africa are 'whites only'. The Communist world's propagandists could hardly ask for a more powerful argument against South Africa and its Western supporters.

"Even some South African whites admit that such facts do enormous damage both to their stance as 'anti-Communist', and to the West's politico-military view of the value of Africa's white south. For the equation suggests that if five people in every six in southern Africa already suffer under a form of oppression remarkably like that inflicted by hard-core communism, this black majority might actually welcome a Communist invasion. 'At least under communism,' said a black South African musician this year, 'I could become conductor of the Pretoria Symphony Orchestra. Under apartheid, the job is whites-only—like every other good South African job from state president down.'

"The all-white government's usual answer to this is to point to its black 'homelands' policy—fragments of South Africa allotted to blacks but on the basis of 28 times more land for a white man than for a black. The blacks' existing South African citizenship is being revoked to 'persuade' them to become citizens of these poor rural reserves—rather like the US government depriving all Americans with Mexican names of their US citizenship, and telling them to live in Mexico. Significantly, the Transkei and Bophuthatswana—sole Bantustans so far to get their alleged independence—are already proving no more independent from South Africa than Czechoslovakia and Poland are from Russia. So even South Africa's Bantustan policy has a distinctly Red tinge.

"It is true that a capitalist, free-enterprise state operating Communist-style laws and labour systems presents quite a paradox. But some South African economists have shown the key to lie in the country's entrenched racism. It is the whites (plus white businessmen, tourists and journalists from overseas) who enjoy the free-enterprise economy. It is the whites' black labour force which is controlled by Communist methods. Apartheid keeps not only the races separate in South Africa : whites and non-whites live under totally different economic and political systems, too—with the whites always on top. Apartheid may quite literally be South Africa's own Iron Curtain.

"If true, this leaves South Africa's anti-Communist stance— favourite theme in the country's multi-million dollar propaganda campaigns in America and Europe—looking rather like the Emperor's New Clothes in the fable. But it might also be asked : 'What does South Africa mean by communism?' For it was as far back as 1962 that an American journalist, covering riots in Johannesburg, described the average South African's view of communism as 'completely screwball'. He seems to have had good cause for his remark.

"In South Africa, most things which offend the extreme Puritanism of the Calvinist government are tarred as 'Communist'. Mini-skirts, dance music on Sundays, pop groups, denim jeans and even television have all at times been classed as 'tools of communism'. Blacks who openly resent white minority rule of their country are quickly labelled Communist or Marxist, and even the one-time editor of Johannesburg's respectable *Rand Daily Mail* was once publicly denounced on the government-controlled radio as 'sharing the propaganda band-wagon with Radio Moscow'—simply for criticizing the government.

"Much more serious—and a fact extensively hidden from the West by South Africa—is that the authorities and indeed the laws equate communism with liberalism and multi-racialism, as in : 'Its major task will be to fight liberalism and communism, and eliminate humanism root and branch' (South African Minister of Education, announcing a new whites-only Johannesburg university).

"South Africa's Suppression of Communism Act, which abolished *Habeas Corpus*, once even imprisoned an anti-Communist Catholic priest without trial, because the Act made 'furthering an aim of communism' a criminal offence—then classed multi-racialism and even spontaneous public protests against apartheid as 'aims of communism'. But those government policies which really do have a Communist flavour, such as exploited labour, forcible relocation of whole black communities and massive restrictions on black personal liberties—plus the administrative apparatus of a police state—instead are officially called 'Christian Nationalism'.

"The effect of these 'Christian' policies today could offer an illuminating eye-opener to the West. For the five-in-six black majority of the population of South Africa has seen again and again that those whites who are anti-racist, fully democratic, courageous and helpful are called 'Communist' by the government and imprisoned, harassed, exiled and deported. So the blacks have come to view sympathy for, and help in their sufferings under, apartheid, as a characteristic of communism. Putting all the facts together, communism looks attractive indeed. And it is the South African government that has made it so.

" 'Most of my people now feel that the Communist devil they don't know can't possibly be as bad as the Apartheid devil they do know,' warned a powerful Zulu chief after the Soweto shootings. And with a recent poll showing that 83 per cent of black South Africans (i.e., 60 per cent of the total South African population) would not resist a Communist invasion, it does indeed seem that white South Africa has, in effect, become the Kremlin's best friend in Africa. And that further Western support for the ruling white minorities in southern Africa may well play straight into Russia's hands by positioning capitalism as racist, and worse than communism, in the minds of much of the Third World."

Since this article was written, ever more extensive mass arrests, closing of newspapers and restrictions even on the white minority's personal freedom have taken place in South Africa, including the "interrogation" to death of Steve Biko (whose own writings prove his anti-Communist outlook, but who has since been tarred as a shrewd Communist agent by a variety of overt and covert South African government sources). Not surprisingly, both black and white anti-apartheid spokesmen in South Africa have warned that the government's actions and attitudes are turning black militants who were originally anti-Communist into Communist sympathizers (for they are called "Communist" whatever they do). The government's only reaction has been to welcome such warnings as further "proof" that anyone opposing apartheid is by definition a communist.

PART THREE

THE EFFECTS

CHAPTER NINE

Black and White: the Empathy Barrier

"I am confident that if the people of the West were exposed to the full realities of southern Africa—to the pervasive evils of racism, of poverty, of torture, of exploitation, of human degradation in all its ugly forms—that they themselves would in revulsion demand their eradication."—*The Secretary-General of the British Commonwealth, speaking in Surrey in July 1978 to the annual meeting of the British Zambia Society.* (The newspaper belatedly reporting this speech noted that in the rest of Britain's media, it had apparently gone unreported.)

I F CERTAIN VITAL facts about South Africa may briefly be restated: South African racism is based on a very simple principle. Using exactly the same criteria by which mediaeval aristocracies preserved their positions of unearned privilege, South Africa insists that the most important thing about a human being is who his parents are. If they are both racially pure white, then the person concerned is accepted into the privileged white-minority society in South Africa and may live, work and buy property there, even if he has just arrived from Patagonia and speaks none of the languages of South Africa.

But if even one of those parents was not wholly white, then the rules of animal pedigree apply—the person is tacitly classed as inferior and must in large measure live where he is told to, is barred from better-paid jobs, is wholly or largely forbidden to own property, and may never become a South African citizen and vote—even if he, and his parents, and their parents for centuries back were all actually born in South Africa.

White South Africa is thus a self-elected aristocracy—but harsher than any normal aristocracy, for even under the most rigid system of nobles and serfs a peasant woman can enter the aristocracy by marriage. In South Africa, even that is barred under the Prohibition of Mixed Marriages Act. South Africa is therefore unique, because it is the only modern state where the oppressed cannot under any circumstances escape from oppression. To this total oppression, an internationally known black personality put the reaction of many of the victims of apartheid quite succinctly some years ago, when he observed : "If someone is standing on your foot, and they keep ignoring your requests to get off, then eventually you just have to hit them—hard."

Obvious though such statements are, the great majority of the world's white people have never fully understood their real implications because, to whites, "racism" nearly always means whites oppressing blacks. So rarely is a white person subjected to life-long racial oppression by blacks that even many liberally-minded whites have no real conception of what racism actually is. And having no real conception of what it is, they have little direct understanding of the depths of the humiliation and frustrations which such people as the blacks of South Africa feel every day of their lives.

The point has an importance beyond mere words. Since the white West is generally unable to understand the enormity of apartheid in South Africa as felt by its victims, it constantly underestimates the size and danger of the racial explosion that may one day come in that part of the world. In fact, many of the free world's newspapers still carry articles claiming that racial oppression is not necessarily any worse than political or religious oppression. Even the partly-liberal *Guardian*, in London, on 17 May 1978 carried a leading article which claimed that it was an example of "double standards" to pretend that there was any difference at all, as far as human rights are concerned, between Russian communism and South African apartheid. Such writers have apparently not fully understood that a man can change both his politics and his religion, but never his race. Racial tyranny is therefore total tyranny. And in a race war, each individual is committed and has his side chosen for him before he is even born—by the colour of his parents' skins. To claim that such an individual has just as many rights under a racial tyranny as he does under a political tyranny (where he can at least change sides) is to misunderstand not only the nature of racism, but the depth of feeling about it amongst black Africans, most of whom—individually or collectively—have felt its lash. For such black feelings can be strong indeed.

Might this be one reason for what the white West feels is

the over-reactive response by black African states at the UN to matters involving Rhodesia and South Africa? Perhaps it is. To explore just one of the avenues opened up by this conjecture, take the instant "kith and kin" reaction amongst white Britons to the murder of whites by blacks in southern Africa. At the time of writing, no such incident has yet reached the deathroll of blacks at Sharpeville or Soweto, or in several incidents involving the deaths of blacks at white hands in and around Rhodesia. But the publicity and public outrage expressed in Britain—and sometimes America and Europe—at such white deaths has at times been enormous, and white attitudes in the West have measurably hardened against black Africa.

But when black attitudes at the UN similarly harden against the white West when even greater numbers of blacks are killed by whites in Africa, the West has been known to accuse black Africa of misusing the UN, and of a vendetta against the West. But might not blacks be in reality feeling a similar "kith and kin" reaction to that which whites feel in similar circumstances? (Further proof of blacks' and whites' common humanity?)

The whites' lack of empathy with the blacks whose countries they are occupying in southern Africa—whether directly or indirectly—may quite possibly be a major, if largely unsuspected factor, in the escalating racial confrontation in that part of the world. Yet even those to whom empathetic understanding is a stranger might gain a glimpse of what is really involved not by trying to see apartheid through blacks' eyes, but by simply reversing apartheid and looking at it through their own white eyes.

Thus, it is not beyond the bounds of most people's imaginations for a white Briton, for instance, to picture a Britain conquered by a black minority from Africa with superior weapons. Although the descendants of these black conquerers still make up only seventeen per cent of Britain's population, they occupy all the seats in parliament and refuse to give white Britons the vote, claiming that only blacks can be true Britons.

They are so rigidly exclusive that they forbid whites to intermarry with them, force whites to live in bleak concrete settlements outside the main cities, use not tear-gas but guns—even on white children—when whites revolt against their treatment, and send "superfluous" whites off to alleged "whitestans" in Yorkshire, Wales and Dartmoor, where they must negotiate

Work Contracts with their black masters before again being allowed to live and work in most of their own country, whose citizenship is steadily being taken away from them by these black latecomers.

It should not be necessary to spell out the whole analogy of a Britain under black apartheid rule, although it is a quite educative exercise to do so. But if one can also imagine in this reversed apartheid situation that this ruling black minority in Britain is spending millions of pounds every year in telling the world how well they are looking after, and "very generously" helping, the white British majority whose country they have taken and settled in, then one can perhaps also begin to imagine the explosive realities behind the image of southern Africa popularly accepted by the white West.

(If the picture is still a little blurred, it could be suggested that one put oneself in the place of a white Briton in a black-ruled Britain who has just been handed this note by a black official: "You are hereby notified that you will be resettled to your local Industrial Estate Compound (single-sex hostel accommodation) on Thursday the 29th day of November, this year. Transport will be available for yourself and your personal belongings such as mattress, suitcase and blankets. Please note: *no* furniture. NB. Your housing permit will be cancelled as from the above-mentioned date, and as your room will be demolished on that date, you are requested to move all your belongings as early as possible." This is in reality a typical eviction notice handed by white township supervisors to black township residents in South Africa. This one was actually issued by the (all white) West Rand Administrative Board, Transvaal, to a black township resident on 9 November 1977.)

Similarly trenchant analogies can be drawn without the need to exercise one's imagination at all. An Indian professional man commented in one of Britain's minority-group magazines in the mid-1970s: "A racist is very simply defined. It is a white Englishman who denies the right of an Indian settler in Britain to bring all the members of his family with him, while defending the right of an English settler in Rhodesia to take all the members of his family with *him*." The converse, of course, is equally true. But the message rarely gets across. 2 October 1978 saw a writer in the London *Daily Telegraph* seriously asserting in a long article that because they brought certain skills with them, the white minority properly "owns" Rhodesia. And even greater confusion of thought was shown in a Conservative amendment to the Queen's Opening of Parliament Speech in November 1978, which described black Rhodesian guerrillas—who are demonstrably more Rhodesian than the white Rhodesian minority—as "alien forces attacking Her Majesty's subjects in Rhodesia".

None of this is to suggest that blacks and Left-wing politicians do not also suffer extreme confusion on racial matters. But the point is that such persistent and often hostile anti-black bias even in allegedly liberal Britain gives a clear hint of overall white racial attitudes in the West; attitudes which not only help increase the white/black polarization and confrontation in southern Africa, but do domestic race relations no good at all.

Most books about South Africa conclude with the author offering a guess of some kind about the future of that country. Where such forecasts have almost always fallen down has been the assumption by the author concerned that he or she knows what the black South African majority will or will not do in the future. For, unarmed though they may be at present, the future does lie largely in their hands. They are the majority. It is their country.

Apart from the indications offered throughout this book of the facts which have most probably shaped current black South African attitudes, this author admits that South Africa's future is as dark to him as it is to most other people. But the West's plans for Africa are susceptible of a rather more specific, if largely tragic forecast, simply because of the West's attitudes.

As President Nyerere of Tanzania has often pointed out, in the early 1960s when he asked the West for help in building a vital railway, he was ignored. But when he got the Chinese to build it, the West accused him of selling out to communism. "Is my country to do without a railway just to please the West?" he later asked. His complaint is now being echoed even more strongly in black countries such as Angola, which once tacitly warned other black African states that the white West's concepts of freedom and democracy in black Africa seem based on the rule that black countries can have any government they like—provided Pretoria and Washington approve of it first. Sarcasm with a grain of truth, perhaps.

From the point of view of the average white Westerner,
persuaded by his country's mass media to see black Africa
mainly in terms of the benefits its minerals and cheap labour
can offer the West, such sharp opinions must seem unnecessarily
hostile and even untrue. But from the point of view of the
average black man in southern Africa, aware of that area's
history of white pillage and oppression, opinions like this are
but the plain truth. The white man has already taken hundreds
of thousands of square miles of land, and billions of dollars'
worth of gold, diamonds and strategic minerals from their
original black owners in black Africa. The idea that the white
West might now be planning to seriously support only those
African states (including South Africa) which show a good
rating in the West's stock exchanges, and to destabilize those
(such as Angola) which do not, is only too believable. For the
black man has seen it all before. But now, at least, in extremis
he has his own ultimate weapon : Russia and Cuba. And it is
precisely because Cuba, in particular, has shown itself willing
to help fight aggressive Western interests in southern Africa,
that Cuba is seen as less of a bogyman than as a friend.

Such is the basic state of play in relation to southern Africa
at the time of writing. On the one side, a white Western world
whose influence today is not entirely negative and whose fumb-
ling attempts to bring true freedom to oppressed blacks are both
recognized and appreciated, but whose viewpoint on Africa in
general is so narrowly restricted by skin colour, education and
history, that only an insignificant percentage of Western whites
glimpse the realities of Africa as Africa's own people see them.
On the other side, is a black African world still partly under
white economic domination, muddling its own inexperienced
way to freedom, and understandably sensitive to outside interference—whether from the West or Russia—which in any way
reminds it of the excesses of colonial days.

And always, there is South Africa. Shrewdly pushing its own
white supremacist views in the West's corridors of power;
claiming to "know what the black man wants"; pretending that
its government has always been a true friend of the free world,
and that the only real enemy in Africa is communism. And thus
perhaps acting as a Judas goat, leading both the East and the
West into a possibly major conflict in, or because of, Africa; a
conflict which South Africa almost seems eager to bring about,

because in October 1978 it threatened that if sanctions were applied against it, South Africa would destabilize the Third World by undercutting world mineral prices, and that this would be done by cutting the already low wages of its black miners. A double blackmail threat aiding the cause not of peace, but of war. Yet it would be a war which the ascertainable human realities of Africa show to be totally unnecessary.

That the West has not ascertained those realities before making its plans for Africa—and particularly for southern Africa —is largely a tribute to the success of South African lobbying and propaganda. To recapitulate :

For many years, South Africa has been strenuously engaged in two sometimes unsuspected activities : the creation and "selling" to the West of a "positive" white-oriented image of the internal situation in South Africa, and the selling of a similarly white-oriented image of Africa as a whole and South Africa's rôle in it, and in Western strategy generally. So success-ful has been this exercise in mass persuasion that, with the help of the residual racial bias of the white West—a hangover from colonial days—South Africa has to a great extent influenced the West to view affairs in Africa only through white eyes, and to put white politics, white feelings and white interests foremost.

Where its own internal affairs are concerned, South Africa has persuaded the conservative West that apartheid is merely "separate development"; that there is some justification and even merit in the black "homelands" policy; that equal pay for equal work, and the carrying out of various improvements, and black self-administration in Soweto and other black ghettos will make apartheid acceptable; that agitation by blacks in South Africa is always Communist-inspired; and that South Africa is rich, stable and a reliable field for investment.

Strategically, South Africa's view of itself is that of a civilized white bastion against communism in Africa; an essential source of minerals needed by the West; a strategic staging-post the West cannot ignore; and a willing and reliable ally in the West's fight against communism world-wide. A picture tacitly accepted today by a wide spectrum of white Western governments.

Yet it is a picture based on a viewpoint as narrow as one which sees all North American affairs only through the eyes of dark-skinned Mexicans, or all European affairs only through the eyes of black Frenchmen. For it ignores the history, feelings, problems, aims and political desires of a mass of people 50 times the size of the white settler-origin communities in Africa—the indigenous black Africans themselves. And their genuinely African viewpoint of the true realities of white interference in their affairs is so far removed from the view on which the white West bases its economic plans for Africa, that few governmental or media sources in the West have yet begun to grasp the size of the gulf between the two. The following paragraphs may possibly help.

South Africa itself, for instance, from the point of view of the great majority of its people, is less a wealthy modern country than a land whose original owners have been deprived of both their country and their birthright, by a white minority which now calls itself "white Africans" but which still labels park benches "Europeans only". A land where every facet of a black man's life is controlled by whites, or by blacks who have the approval of whites. Where the blacks' original societies were destroyed by alien whites. Where the British Commonwealth citizenship which the blacks later enjoyed was arbitrarily removed from them in 1961 by a decision taken solely by whites. Where even the blacks' citizenship of the land of their birth—South Africa— is now being steadily stripped from them, without their permission or consent, by whites whose roots are not even in Africa, but 6,000 miles away in Europe. And where almost everything that makes life worth living to an ordinary human being—the right to fair and equal education, housing, jobs, medical facilities and travel, and the opportunity to strive for the highest positions in business, science, commerce, the arts and government in their own country—is permanently denied to them; so that to a growing number of blacks communism, with its talk of equality and opportunity, is a thing not to be feared but perhaps to welcome with a hunger created by generations of frustration and exploitation. And it is this deep and strong determination to be free of apartheid domination which is most likely to determine South Africa's future.

Thus, many may not wait for outside deliverance, but may create their own. Already in South Africa the internal guerrilla war has started, and it is again significant that the mass media of the West have almost totally ignored it—many people in Britain first learning of it in a May 1978 television interview

with Mr Vorster in which the interviewer pointed out that for
months past there had been an average of one bomb explosion
every five days in South Africa (a fact hidden both from
intending tourists and potential immigrants).

But it is the next stage which white South Africa most fears,
yet is careful never to mention. For the very race of people
which white South Africa has rejected, exploited, segregated
and tacitly classed as an inferior species, works and in many
cases actually lives in and around almost every white South
African home in the entire country : the black domestic servant.
The person who cleans the house, makes the beds, and does the
gardening.

This is one of the great anomalies of the whole apartheid
policy, and largely accounts for the whites' increasing feeling of
vulnerability. For the black and white populations of South
Africa are physically intermeshed. Even a very small black
rebellion would probably include blacks already inside the very
homes of the whites. Yet the effects of even a minor "rebellion"
by such black South Africans would be incalculable. For white
South Africa would then have to decide which is the more
important—personal safety, or cheap domestic labour. The
Catch-22 situation being simply that without the high standard
of living and physical comfort which ample black domestic
labour provides for almost all white South African families,
South Africa is a much less desirable place for whites to live in,
and many would certainly emigrate, increasing the feelings of
isolation and tension amongst those left behind.

The indigenous black viewpoint of the historical and current
situation in much of the rest of Africa is more complex, but its
basic theme is similar to South Africa's.

In Mozambique and Angola, for instance, the simplistic
Western view of the affairs of southern Africa in terms of the
West versus Russia and Cuba is viewed by many blacks either
with astonishment, or as final proof of Western cynicism and/or
deviousness. It is not intended to defend such black views here,
but simply to list the historical facts of which they are the
logical outcome.

In both Mozambique and Angola, roughly 400 years of
Portuguese rule—which as recently as the early 1970s included
practices classed by the UN as slavery—finally produced viable
black-resistance movements. The two most important, the MPLA

and FRELIMO, appealed to the white West for help but were ignored. America, in particular, wanted strategic military use of the Azores, and refused to do anything to upset the Portuguese. The resistance movements then successfully turned to the only other source of help—the Communist world, and inevitably became largely communist themselves.

Before the Portuguese capitulated in 1974, FRELIMO found not only that there was a white plan to bring one million Portuguese settlers into Mozambique to help crush black resistance movements for all time, but it also found itself fighting white South African troops, invited in by the colonial authorities to help subdue FRELIMO in Tete Province. To the black people of Mozambique, then, white capitalist régimes are understandably equated with the conquest of black peoples' countries, the enslavement of their black inhabitants and the refusal to give even medical aid in a "just war" against racial oppression. The Communists, on the other hand, are seen as deliverers. For they gave help.

The experience of the black Angolans has been even worse. Again, the white West originally refused all help, but after the MPLA were forced to turn to Russia for arms and medical supplies, the West-backed state of Zaire began to support a rival Angolan resistance group, the FNLA, and white South Africa backed yet another group, UNITA, thus making civil war inevitable when the Portuguese left.

With the American CIA bringing in arms for the FNLA in 1975, and South Africa invading Angola in depth from the south, the MPLA called in Cuba, eventually won the war, and was recognized as the sovereign government of Angola. South Africa, forced to withdraw, immediately began to destabilize Angola by pouring men and arms into southern Angola to help the shattered remnants of UNITA. In the meantime, the Angolans had openly put on trial certain white British mercenaries who had been fighting against them during the civil war, and were astonished to find even the Left-wing British Labour government describing the court's verdicts as "shocking". Black Angolans were not slow to notice that no such expressions of distaste were forthcoming from Britain when, in May 1978, South Africa again invaded their country and killed not only SWAPO guerrillas, but 400 unarmed black women, children and babies. Their view of Western morality was not improved when in the same month the American President announced that America might soon arm the UNITA rebels in order to help destroy the recognized Angolan government, thus handing the Communist world a powerful propaganda weapon in Africa. (In the event, America in this case saw the dangers in time.)

The same pattern of behaviour has been noted by the indigenous peoples of South West Africa, now Namibia. The original German settlers in the nineteenth century used at times to hang whole groups of local inhabitants when it was thought that an example should be set, and in some cases a policy of genocide was pursued.[1] In 1919 the territory was given by the League of Nations to South Africa to "bring to self-determination". The exploitation of the blacks continued, and in 1948 South Africa introduced apartheid.

By the 1960s mass trials were being illegally conducted in Pretoria by the South African government, of native Namibians who complained about racist South African rule in their country. In 1964 Bantustans were set up by South Africa in Namibia, under which the 90,000 white-settler minority gave itself two-thirds of all the land, including two-thirds of the total arable land, and almost all the diamond and uranium deposits, while the 800,000 indigenous inhabitants got the rest—most of it desert. A discrimination of nearly twenty to one against the blacks in land share—not very different from that in South Africa.

In 1966 the United Nations ruled South Africa's presence in Namibia illegal, and in 1971 the International Court of Justice confirmed this illegality. South Africa ignored both bodies and began to build up Namibia as a military outpost of South Africa, continuing to use the black inhabitants as cheap labour in order to make huge profits for white South Africa from Namibia's mineral resources. In 1975, South Africa launched its own private invasion of Angola from the UN territory of Namibia.

By the same year, however, it was becoming clear to South Africa that it must make other arrangements about Namibia, and on 25 May 1975 Mr Vorster publicly announced that "We do not claim for ourselves one single inch of South West Africa's soil."

Mid-1978 was marked by a massive and well-financed white propaganda campaign in Namibia to persuade the inhabitants

7—   • •

to elect a pro-South African government, coupled with arrests by the white South African police of the leaders of the main political party representing Namibian—as distinct from South African—interests.

Again, one sees that viewed from the standpoint of the majority of Namibians, white capitalism has meant murder, slave labour, near-genocide, the theft of their land and the arrest and imprisonment, over a long period of time, of their leaders. Facts to which much of the white West still closes its eyes.

And finally, Rhodesia. It is less than 100 years since an armed column of white South Africans entered that country, negotiated some land from Chief Lobengula, then later ignored the agreement and took all the land and minerals that they desired. The nature of the white rule that developed can be seen in such officially documented facts as the black death-rate in the white man's Rhodesian mines between 1900 and 1933, when no less than 30,000 blacks died from unnatural causes including accidents, assaults by white officials, malnutrition and venereal diseases induced by the mines' system of official black prostitution to keep their labour force quiet, and from which the white mining officials got a cut of the profits.[2]

Recent Rhodesian events are more generally known. They can be summed up briefly : a land-apportionment system giving whites, *per capita*, more than twenty times more land than blacks (almost identical to South African land discrimination); the hi-jacking of the almost voteless black majority into an illegal white-ruled state in 1965; the bringing in of white South African troops between 1967 and 1975 to help kill dissident blacks; the imprisonment of black leaders without trial; the West's breaking of oil sanctions; and the standard Rhodesian practice after guerrilla battles of treating white corpses with reverence and respect, but of displaying black corpses like dead animals in the towns as a "warning" of what it meant in Rhodesia to dispute white rule, whether direct or indirect.

In Rhodesia, too, the nations of the West showed their true racial standards. Only after whites began to be killed did either America or Britain show any real interest in bringing illegal white Rhodesian rule to an end—but not by force; by protracted discussions instead. Perhaps the entire situation, from the indigenous blacks' point of view, was summed up by an African writing in *The Guardian* in June 1978. He pointed out that the recent killing of 200 whites in Zaire had produced not only instant armed help from France and Belgium, but rapid plans for both a black African security force in Africa and a major white mercenary army to be stationed mainly in Zaire itself. But the black death-roll of nearly 10,000 as a result of Rhodesia's illegal UDI, plus the two lethal South African invasions of Angola, the illegal South African annexation of Namibia and the killings of hundreds of black South African schoolchildren by white police at Soweto had produced no help for blacks at all—nor even a hint of such help—from the white West. Not surprisingly, a growing proportion of blacks is now convinced that the white West sees them as expendable.

The above facts may appear to have been set down in somewhat trenchant language, but this is simply because this is how much of the black population of Africa sees such facts. Yet the West has repeatedly evaded the issue and instead has behaved as if the only enemy the 250 million or so black Africans have to be afraid of is some "Communist" weapons in Angola and the Horn of Africa, and a few thousand Cubans, the very mention of whose name appears to trigger some kind of panic in many Western quarters. And so, not very surprisingly, many thoughtful Africans see the West—and America and France in particular—not merely as cynically anti-black, but as extremely poorly informed.

Yet it may be apparent from the contents of this book alone that a realistic, perhaps non-violent and substantially pro-West solution to the affairs of southern Africa seems to be for the West to put its money where its mouth is, and for once support the principles of freedom and democracy in southern Africa. This means pre-empting and under-cutting the temptations of communism by actually supporting the original and majority owners of southern Africa—the blacks. It means giving honest help, without strings, to all black-ruled states in southern Africa —because this may well offer the greatest probability of success in bringing such states into the Western orbit as genuine friends, who will then be prepared to offer their strategic minerals to the West at a fair price. But above all, it means that the West, after pretending to despise apartheid for so many years while actually quietly profiting from that anti-black practice, must at last confront white South Africa—not only for the blacks' sake, but for the whites' as well.

More than ten years ago, this author suggested in a book that because the whites of South Africa have so much to lose, in a major military confrontation they might not fight—or not fight for long. This view is now gaining further support in some quarters in the West.[3] But a military confrontation with South Africa is, in fact, an open admission of failure to simply sit down and think about the problem. For the solution could be quite simple.

South Africa has been accusing the West of double standards for so long, that it could be time to call the bluff. And one way to call it is simply to take white South Africa at its word when it says that "separate development" is neither racism nor discrimination, and to apply South Africa's apartheid laws against apartheid's creators—South Africa's white people; not necessarily collectively, but certainly individually.

For instance, it would certainly be preferable to a race war in southern Africa (which could hardly help race relations elsewhere in the world) for the outside world instead to apply these white-created South African laws against white South Africans travelling outside their country.

Accommodation: Only a limited number of hotels in the world's capital cities to take white South Africans, almost all other hotels—including those in major resorts—to be closed to them. When citizens of other nations are present, no drinks to be served to white South Africans in bars or restaurants. (Cf., South African liquor laws forbidding "multi-national" drinking.)

Travel: White South Africans to be required to obtain permits to travel beyond the capital cities in other countries, and to be forbidden to travel first class. All white South Africans to report to the local police at least once every week and advise on their travel plans. (Cf., the Group Areas Act, etc.)

Family travel: South Africans married to persons holding non-South African citizenship to be forbidden to book into the same hotel, or even to kiss or hold hands, during the entire duration of their stay in other countries. (Cf., South African Mixed Marriages Act.)

Sex: White South Africans of either sex to be forbidden to date, make love to, dance with or kiss members of the opposite sex who are not South African citizens. (Cf., South African Immorality Act, Citizenship Acts, etc.)

Entertainment: White South Africans to be given a list of innocuous plays and films in each country they visit, being forbidden to see any other plays or films, or to visit night clubs or any other places of entertainment. (Cf., Group Areas Act.)

Visas: All white South Africans to be politically interrogated before being granted a visa to visit a foreign country, all such visas to be delayed for at least three months before issue. (Cf., treatment of black South Africans applying for South African passports.)

Property: White South Africans to be forbidden to buy property, operate a business, or employ or give orders to other nationals when outside South Africa. (Cf., South African Group Areas Act; Section 77 of Act 28 of 1956; etc.)

Passports: All white South Africans to be required to carry all passports and other travel documents on them at all times, failing which a heavy fine or one month's labour on a local farm to be imposed. (Cf., the South African Pass Laws for blacks.)

The above suggestions might be sufficient for a start. In the event that after a pre-determined time such South African laws were still in operation in South Africa, further "South African" laws could be introduced in foreign countries, such as one forcing all white South Africans owning property or businesses outside South Africa to sell them to local nationals at a stated price. (Cf., South African Group Areas Act, as amended, and as used for instance against Coloured property owners in District Six in Cape Town.)

There seems a very fair probability that it would not be very long before white South Africans, treated by the outside world in much the same way as they themselves treat blacks in South Africa, would capitulate and force their whites-only government to at last dismantle apartheid. Yet if such a plan were in fact put forward, it regrettably seems an absolute certainty that loud voices would be raised in the West, claiming that the whole plan would be both inoperable and inhuman. Yet the whole point is that it already operates in South Africa, against innocent people. And if it is described as inhuman, then must not that same description apply to those who operate and subsidize apartheid, on whose laws this plan is directly and fairly based?

As each South African race law is abandoned, so would each of these overseas laws applying to white South Africans be abandoned—to be instantly reintroduced if the South Africans were found to be insincere or indulging in camouflage. The entire system could be operated without a drop of blood being spilt.

But it must be admitted that the West, for all its talk about the horror of a racial war in southern Africa being "too dreadful to contemplate", would almost certainly never agree to such a plan. Instead, with white South Africa, it will—one fears— go on and on expecting some kind of miracle which will somehow erode away apartheid without eroding away the West's apartheid-derived profits from South Africa. Until it is too late.

Until black South Africa does go violently and voluntarily Communist. Until a black-resistance movement does arise with really tight security in South Africa—with some of its members actually employed within white South Africa's homes, and in many essential services. Or until South Africa's leaders, with their background of wartime treachery and their hard core of religious zealots who believe that everything they do is "the Will of God", light a nuclear fuse in southern Africa and put all the world in peril. For only the heavily blinkered still pretend that South Africa does not have nuclear weapons and would not hesitate to use them.

True, these are but possibilities. But that they are in fact possible at all is a factor which should enter into any Western government's—and every multi-national corporation's—equations for their future policy towards minority white rule in the southern part of an undeniably black continent. For if the author of this book were to risk a prophecy, it would be that the West will, in the days ahead, take the morally wrong and economically wrong decisions, yet again. That step by step, it will evade the facing of facts and avoid the temporarily hard options of bloodless short cuts to the erasing of apartheid, until everything has got out of hand. And then—based on close observation of the gap between southern African facts and the West's version of those facts, and the West's usual behaviour when suddenly faced with realities it has long ignored—the West could over-react, and start blaming either the Communists or black Africa itself, egged on by white South Africa and its influential fellow-travellers in Britain, Europe and America.

What happens then is probably anybody's guess. But it does seem that such an apocalyptic sequence of events is unnecessary, and with a little courage can still be avoided.

One more question needs to be asked. Even those whose opinions or experience leads them to disagree extensively with the contents of this book, might admit that the variety of facts it presents prove that South African affairs are frequently quite seriously misreported in the West. Yet South Africa is a country where English is spoken almost everywhere, where there has been for some years a larger cadre of foreign journalists and observers than perhaps any other country of comparable size in the world, and where more British companies have investments and branches and which more British MPs have visited than any other country, perhaps, outside Europe.

And yet despite all this, many experts appear once again to have got it wrong. How much reliance, then, can be placed on the mass media's statements (and politicians' comments) about all those other countries, from Tanzania to Korea, where no such intimate daily contact with the West's politicians, multinationals and mass media exist? Just how accurate *is* the picture the public of the free world's countries gets of the rest of the world?

APPENDIX

South Africa in Figures

Land shares

Total area : 472,000 square miles.

Population : Total :   26.5 million
(1978)   Blacks :   19 million 72%
        Whites :   4.3 million 16%
        Coloureds : 2.4 million 9%
        Asians :   800,000 ... ... 3%

Area reserved by whites for black occupation : 13.7% = 65,000 sq. miles.

Area reserved by whites for white occupation : 86% = 405,000 sq. miles.

Area reserved by whites for Coloured and Asian occupation : less than 1,000 sq. miles (no "homelands" have been set aside for Coloureds or Asians).

Land share by race :
    $10\frac{1}{2}$ whites per sq. mile (60 acres for each white).
    290 blacks per sq. mile (2.2 acres for each black).

—That is, each white, under the white-created "homelands" policy, gets on average 28 times more land than each black.

Income shares

1978 incomes, by race, per person per year (extrapolated from Chapter 4 and later data from reliable sources, and thus close approximations only) :

Whites : R3,800   Asians : R800   Coloureds : R600   Blacks : R220

Some *per capita* incomes in Africa (converted to rands), per annum, 1973 (latest reported figures, provided for comparison purposes in view of standard white South African claim that black South Africans "have the highest incomes of blacks in Africa").

White South Africans :	R2,200
Black South Africans :	R135
*Zambians :	R270
Ethiopians :	R60
*Congolese :	R245
Tanzanians :	R65

*Ivory Coast :	R340
Zaireans :	R75
*Nigerians :	R155

(Asterisked figures are from a Markinor professional survey, quoted in the *Rand Daily Mail*, Johannesburg, on 30 November 1974. Other African figures are from South African propaganda literature. South African figures : Senbank, etc.)

A comparison of some ratios of discrimination
Against blacks by whites in southern Africa (all figures *per capita*).
Land Share : South Africa—whites 28 times more than blacks.
　　　　　　 Rhodesia—whites 19 times more than blacks.
　　　　　　 Namibia—whites nearly 20 times more than blacks.
Education expenditure : South Africa—whites 16.5 times more
　(1976)　　　　　　 than blacks.
　　　　　　　　　　 Rhodesia—whites 11.5 times more than
　　　　　　　　　　 blacks.
Incomes : South Africa—whites at least 15 times more than blacks.
　(1977)　 Rhodesia—whites at least 15 times more than blacks.
Doctors : South Africa—approximately 20 times more for whites
　　　　　 than for blacks.
Pensions : South Africa—whites 7 times more than blacks.

A brief but useful non-figure comparison
Between white and black South African rights and life-styles, which can be read in conjunction with the comparison given in the section on Apartheid in Sport :

	Typical white Johannesburger	*Typical black Johannesburger*
Job :	Clerical worker.	Clerical worker.
Home :	3-bedroom house, nice suburb.	4-roomed hut, Soweto.
Employment :	May employ anybody.	Cannot employ whites.
Opportunities :	Unlimited.	Cannot rise above lowest white, in firm.
Vote :	Full vote for Central Govt.	No vote for Central Govt.
Laws :	Citizen's say in law-making.	No say in law-making.

Property :	May own and speculate.	May not own or speculate.
Passport :	Easy to obtain.	Very difficult to obtain.
Weapons :	May own and carry a gun.	Forbidden to own or carry arms.
Holidays :	Almost anywhere.	Travel and resort restrictions.
Security :	May reside anywhere in South Africa, as of right.	Must live where told; can be instantly deported to Bantustan.
Forebears :	Arrived in Africa 17th-20th century.	Arrived South Africa perhaps 10th century or earlier.

SOURCES AND REFERENCES

Chapter 1: Racial Bias and the Mass Media
1. *Daily Mirror*, London, 24/2/78.
2. *Daily Express*, London, 30/11/77.
3. *The Times*, London, 23/4/74.
4. A documentary on the KGB, highly critical of the Soviet Union.
5. BBC-2 TV, 1/12/77.
6. *Week-end Telegraph*, London, May 1967.

Chapter 2: The South African Propaganda Machine
NB The summary of the revelations of Department of Information abuses of public funds, and its setting up of "front" organizations, etc., is a chronological assessment mainly from the London *Times, Guardian* and *Daily Telegraph,* cross-checked with South African media.
1. *The Great White Hoax*, Africa Bureau, London, 1977.
2. *New Statesman*, London, 16/8/68.
3. *The Guardian, The Times, Daily Telegraph*, London, 17/4/78.
4. *To the Point*, Johannesburg, 26/5/78 and *The Guardian*, London, 6/6/78.
5. *Sunday Times*, London, 23/4/78.
6. Ibid., 3/11/68.

Chapter 3: The Basic Historical Deception
1. Policy statement, 22/9/66.
2. "Some Recent Radiocarbon Dates from Eastern and Southern Africa", by Dr T. Maggs, Natal Museum, South Africa, *Journal of African History*, Cambridge University Press, Vol. XVIII, No. 2.
3. Ibid., and *Southern Africa in the Iron Age*, Prof. B. Fagan, Thames & Hudson, 1965.
4. *The Cambridge History of Africa*, Vol. III, 1977, *et al.*
5. *A Tour in South Africa*, Freeman, London, 1890(?), *et al.*
6. *A History of Southern Africa*, Eric Walker, London, 1959.
7. Other material used in British and American schools also carries the falsified version of South African history (e.g., Sterling Publishing Company's "Visual Geography" series) but it is not suggested that any such material knowingly carries such misinformation.

8. Generally reported in the British and South African press, in April 1978.
9. Extensive, documented evidence will be found in *Divide and Rule—South Africa's Bantustans*, Barbara Rogers, D & A Fund, London, 1976.

Chapter 4: Job Reservation and the Income Gap
Section one: Job Reservation:
1. *Emigrating to South Africa*, printed and published in Britain.
2. *Daily Telegraph*, London, 31/8/77.
3. Quoted from the official South African embassy transcript.
4. From the South African parliamentary record, esp. May and September.
5. It can happen that whites may accept, voluntarily, some orders from blacks, as in the case of white journalists working under the black editor of the black (but white-owned) *Post* newspaper. But the whites retain the right to refuse to obey such orders, without jeopardizing their position. Blacks however must by law obey orders given by whites.
6. *Sunday Times*, London, 23/10/77.
7. The South African embassy in the *Financial Times*, London, 15/9/77.
8. *To The Point*, Johannesburg, 9/1/78.

Section two: the Black/White Income Gap:
1. *Financial Times*, London, 27/1/78, letter from South African embassy, for example.
2. 2/12/65.
3. 15/9/77.
4. 19/12/77, in *To The Point*, Johannesburg.
5. *The Guardian*, London, 23/3/76.
6. *Financial Times*, London, 27/1/78.
7. *Rand Daily Mail*, Johannesburg, 2/2/75.
8. *To The Point*, Johannesburg, 30/6/78.
9. *Financial Mail*, Johannesburg, 13/10/72.
10. All these figures were published as a special Fact Sheet in Britain in 1975 by the Africa Bureau, London.
11. South African embassy transcript, London, 6/5/77.
12. "Race Relations and the South African economy", quoting Bureau of Statistics data for 1973.

Chapter 5: Apartheid in Medicine, Education and Sport
1. "A Survey of Race Relations in South Africa", Johannesburg, 1972, quoting the Minister for National Education; Medical

Association of South Africa, in *Report from South Africa,* Vol. 12, No. 5, South African embassy, London; South African Government Department of Labour and Manpower Survey, No. 10, 1973.

2. *The Times,* London, 13/3/69.
3. UN, "Notes and Documents", 26/71, June 1971.
4. *Man Alive,* BBC-2, 12/12/74.
5. *Race Relations News,* Johannesburg, March 1971. Seven years later the *Star,* Johannesburg, confirmed that the mortality rate was still very high with the comment that South Africa is "a country where malnutrition is a major killer of blacks" (*New African,* London, November 1978).
6. *The History of South Africa,* Prof. G. Were, Evans Ltd, 1974. Also article, Scully and van der Merwe, in *World Archaeology,* October 1971.
7. *Report from South Africa,* South African embassy, London, April 1972.
8. *Rand Daily Mail,* Johannesburg, 25 and 29/6/73.
9. *Forbidden Pastures,* F. Troup, D & A Fund, London, 1976, p. 39.
10. *Sports Illustrated,* USA, June 1969, article by Tex Maule.
11. *The Guardian,* London, 12/10/76.
12. Ibid., 25/2/78.
13. Ibid., 4/3/78.
14. Ibid., 18/3/78.

Chapter 6: Allies or Enemies of the Free World?

1. *Verwoerd,* Alexander Hepple, Pelican, 1967, p. 211.
2. *The Times,* London, 16/6/42.
3. *Die Transvaler,* Johannesburg, 6/11/40.
4. *Verwoerd,* A. Hepple; and *The Rise of the South African Reich,* B. Bunting, Penguin African Library, 1969.
5. The Nazi laws are as given in *Documents of Nazism,* Noakes & Pridham, 1974.
6. *The Guardian,* London, 14/8/76.
7. *Rand Daily Mail,* Johannesburg, 22/5/65.
8. *New Statesman,* London, 9/12/77.
9. Editor, *Die Transvaler,* Johannesburg, quoted in *Sunday Times,* London, 17/9/78.
10. *Missionary Travels and Researches in South Africa,* New York, 1858.

Chapter 7: South African Interference in Other Countries

1. *Report from South Africa,* South African embassy, London, Jan-June 1975.

2. *Sunday Times*, Johannesburg, 14/11/65.
3. *The Guardian*, London, 14/4/78.
4. *Report from South Africa*, London, July-Dec 1975.
5. Ibid., Jan-June 1975.

Chapter 9: Black and White: the Empathy Barrier
1. A typical "Extermination Order" was reprinted in *Krieg und Frieden im Hererolande*, C. Rust, Berlin, 1905.
2. *Chibaro*, Charles van Onselen, Pluto Press, London, 1976.
3. e.g., in the *New Statesman*, London, 16/6/78.

ANNOTATED BIBLIOGRAPHY

THE MOST USUAL function of a Bibliography in a work of non-fiction is to combine a list of major sources used by the author, with suggestions for further reading. However, complications set in when an author's book is largely devoted to exposing the fact that much commonly accepted—and usually quite innocently accepted—information in articles, speeches and books about his subject is in fact propaganda, biased in favour of one point of view only—in this case that of the white South African minority.

Indeed, the bulk of the "popular" books about South Africa over the past dozen years or so fall clearly into this category. Where they touch on South African history, it is usually the false, pro-apartheid version which is presented, and many other long-discredited white South African propaganda themes from economics to education of the "Bantus" are earnestly presented as "fact" in their pages. Yet such authors are quite honest and sincere. What has happened is that, as whites, they have gone to an African country wholly under the control of a white minority, have mixed almost exclusively with that white minority, have often not understood that any discussions they may have had with members of the black majority have taken place under laws promising severe penalties for "unfair criticism" of apartheid, and have written books which tend to reflect not South Africa, but merely white South Africa. (I was once so deceived myself.)

This bias even finds its way into travel books. This author has, over more than fifteen years, been able to find only one travel book describing South Africa—out of the very many published—which makes clear that for black Britons or Americans, visas to South Africa are difficult to obtain, most hotels, restaurants, cinemas, etc., are closed to blacks, white South Africa's much-praised hospitality does not apply to black tourists, and it can be most upsetting and even dangerous for black tourists to step off the rigid tourist-track and, for instance, visit some of the wholly *verkramp* small towns of the Transvaal and Orange Free State in particular. (The non-racial tourism book is *Travellers' Guide to Africa*, published by International Communications Ltd, London, in 1977; the other travel books consulted—and nearly all published articles on holidays in South Africa—carry information which is true only if read by whites.)

In view of the above factors, this Bibliography has been generally restricted to listing South African propaganda material, plus well-documented, accurate publications about South Africa pertinent to the subjects covered. One useful point can be made about the so-called popular genre of books about South Africa, however, and that is that it has almost always been found that those which carry more than just a few of the propaganda misconceptions detailed earlier in this book, cannot really be considered to be reliable works on the subject, by definition. This group includes not only most books by white visitors to South Africa, but large numbers by white South Africans themselves, however exalted. And as noted in Chapter 2 herein, reference books published in South Africa, even those very few which make an effort to be objective and fair, are by definition pre-censored, under no less than 24 laws covering what may or may not be published in that country.

Where pro-apartheid booklets are concerned, there has been such a worldwide flood of these every year from the South African government and its departments and agencies that only a representative sample will be listed here. These and propaganda magazines can be obtained in English from :

Britain : South African embassy, Trafalgar Square, London WC2.

Canada : South African embassy, 15 Sussex Drive, Ottawa 2, Ontario.

USA : South African embassy, Washington D.C. 20008; and South African Information Service, 655 Madison Ave., N.Y. 10021.

Australia : South African embassy, 3 Zeehan Street, Red Hill, Canberra.

New Zealand : South African consulate, P.O. Box 3750, Wadestown, Wellington.

SOUTH AFRICAN BOOKS AND BOOKLETS DIRECTLY OR
INDIRECTLY DEFENDING APARTHEID
(FH = supports the official, fallacious version of history)

South Africa Year Book, published by the South African government.

Multi-National Development in South Africa—the Reality, Department of Information, Pretoria, 1974. FH. (Also a falsified historical map.)

South Africa—a Skunk Among Nations (the title is sarcastic), by L. de Villiers, at the time second-in-command of South Africa's Department of Information. An angry attack on overseas critics of apartheid. Tandem Press, London, 1975.

The World, the West and Pretoria, by Alexander Steward, one-time Director of Information at the South African embassy, London, and government broadcaster. David McKay Inc., New York, 1977. (In its first few pages this book seriously claims that Jews are "white", but Arabs are "non-white".) FH.

Health and Healing: Hospital and Medical Services for South Africa's Developing Nations, Department of Information, Pretoria, first printed 1969.

This is South Africa, Department of Information, Pretoria, 1975. FH.

Progress Through Separate Development: South Africa in Peaceful Transition, Information Service of South Africa, New York, 1973. FH.

State of South Africa Year Book (annually), da Gama Publications, Johannesburg (but described in some government propaganda literature as an "official reference" work). FH.

Stepping into the Future: education for South Africa's black, Coloured and Indian peoples, Erudita Publications, Johannesburg, 1975. FH. 80,000 copies of this book were bought by the South African government and sent, unsolicited, to schools in several countries including Britain.

(Many other, similar books can be acquired on request at South African embassies listed above.)

SOUTH AFRICAN MAGAZINES AND JOURNALS DEFENDING
APARTHEID, PUBLISHED BY THE SOUTH AFRICAN GOVERNMENT

Bantu, Pretoria, in English. Also distributed overseas.
Comment and Opinion, Pretoria, in English. Also distributed overseas.
South African Digest, Pretoria, in English. Also distributed overseas.
South African Panorama, Pretoria, in English. Also distributed overseas.
South African Panorama, Berne, in French, German, Italian, Portuguese, Spanish and Dutch.
Revue Südafrika, Berne, in German.
Beelden, Brussels, in Dutch.
Images, Brussels, in French.
Service de Presse Sud-Africain, Brussels, in French.
Zuid-Afrikaanse Persdienst, Brussels, in Dutch.
Sud Africa Informa, Buenos Aires, in Spanish.
Journal Südafrika, Bonn, in German.
RSA Pressebericht, Bonn, in German.

South African Review, Canberra, in English.
South African News Release, Canberra, in English.
Noticias da Africa do Sul, Lisbon, in Portuguese.
Noticias de Africa del Sur, Lisbon, in Spanish.
Report from South Africa, London, in English.
South African Press Mirror, London, in English.
South African Scope, New York, in English.
l'Afrique du Sud d'aujourd'hui, Paris, in French.
Sud Africa leri. Oggi. Domani, Rome, in Italian.
Settimana Sudafricana, Rome, in Italian.
Zuidafrikaanse Koerier, The Hague, in Dutch.
Nieuwsbulletin, The Hague, in Dutch.
Heute aus Südafrika, Vienna, in German.
Südafrika Kompass, Vienna, in German.

(The above list of regular magazines published by the South
African government and its embassies is for 1975, a representative
year. Several of these publications consisted of highly selective
press reports. The list is by courtesy of Mr Julian Burgess and the
Africa Bureau, London.)

To The Point International, Johannesburg and Antwerp, weekly.
Privately published, this *Time*-style magazine has stated that it
does not publish South African government propaganda. Its
critics point out the facts that several of its early correspondents
and editors soon became official South African government
propagandists (e.g., its original 1972 assistant editor, Dr Eschel
Rhoodie, became head of the South African Department of
Information), its present editor (1978) was once Director of
Information at the South African embassy, London, and in
1977 five of its Antwerp editors left after stating that the magazine published government propaganda transmitted from Pretoria. This the publishers denied. In fact, the magazine is
written almost solely by whites, and generally supports the South
African *status quo.* Large numbers of copies are sent *gratis*
every week to influential people throughout the world. On
30.4.79, South Africa's Foreign Minister admitted that *To The
Point* magazine had in fact been secretly funded by his government, at the rate of some R1 million per year.

EXTENSIVELY-DOCUMENTED BOOKS CRITICAL OF APARTHEID

A Survey of Race Relations in South Africa (annually), South
African Institute of Race Relations, Johannesburg. (Useful
current data.)

White Laager, Prof. W. H. Vatcher, Praeger Inc., and Pall Mall Press, 1965.

Verwoerd, Alexander Hepple, Pelican, 1967. (General political summary.)

The Rise of the South African Reich, Brian Bunting, Penguin African Library, 1969 (an in-depth examination of the strong links between German nazism and Afrikaner nationalism).

The Discarded People, Father Cosmas Desmond, Penguin African Library, 1971 (detailed facts and eye-witness accounts of the evictions of millions of "superfluous" blacks from so-called "white" South Africa).

The South African Connection, First, Steele & Gurney, Temple Smith, 1972 (British and Western trade links with South Africa, and the nature and effects of apartheid in employment).

The Great White Hoax, Africa Bureau, London, 1977 (general examination of South African external and internal propaganda tactics).

The Defence and Aid Fund of Southern Africa, Amen Court, London E.C.4, regularly publishes carefully-researched booklets on various aspects of South African apartheid. It would be fair to say that these offer the most reliable continuing insight into the realities of southern Africa. Some useful titles include :

Masters and Serfs—farm labour in South Africa, Rosalynde Ainslie, 1973.

A Dwelling Place of our own: the Story of the Namibian Nation, Randolph Vigne, 1973 (essential background reading for understanding Namibia).

Divide and Rule—South Africa's Bantustans, Barbara Rogers, 1976 (probably the definitive account of the political duplicity on which this policy is based).

Forbidden Pastures—education under apartheid, Freda Troup, 1976 (a fruitful contrast to *Stepping into the Future,* listed above).

A Window on Soweto, Joyce Sikakane, 1977 (one of the few published insights into Soweto and apartheid as those who actually live in Soweto know it).

PROFESSIONAL WORKS WHICH ABSOLUTELY REFUTE THE OFFICIAL SOUTH AFRICAN VERSION OF THAT COUNTRY'S HISTORY, on which apartheid and the "homelands" policy is based. It should be noted that these are not political, but thoroughly documented scientific works from a variety of sources, and that they were written not to engage in controversy, but simply to record the facts.

A Historical Geography of the British Colonies, Lucas, London, 1900.

Mapungubwe, L. Fouche, Cambridge University Press, 1937.

The Pre-History of the Transvaal, Prof. R. Mason, Johannesburg, 1962.

Historical Geography of South Africa, Pollock & Agnew, Longmans, 1963.

Southern Africa in the Iron Age, Prof. B. Fagan, Thames & Hudson, 1965.

The Oxford History of South Africa, Vol. I, OUP, 1969.

Archaeology in Southern Africa, H. C. Woodhouse, Purnell (South Africa), 1971.

World Archaeology, article by Scully & van der Merwe, October 1971.

Encyclopaedia Britannica, Vol. XVII, 1974, *et seq.*

The Cambridge History of Africa, Vols. III and IV, CUP, 1977.

South Africa—a Modern History, Prof. T. Davenport, Macmillan (South Africa), 1977.

The Journal of African History, Cambridge University Press, 1977, pp. 161 *et seq.* (The JAH in many issues contains massively documented material proving extensive black occupation of South Africa many centuries before the first whites arrived).

To which could be added the detailed political history of South Africa : *South Africa—an Historical Introduction*, by F. Troup, Eyre Methuen, 1972, which contains also a useful summary of Rhodesia's true history.

USEFUL ADDITIONAL READING

Racism and the Mass Media, Hartmann & Husband, Davis-Poynter, 1974.

O.B.—Traitors or Patriots?, G. C. Visser, Macmillan (South Africa), 1976. (An unusual book which details much hitherto unknown Ossewabrandwag treachery in World War II, but tends to ignore the most important source-book on the subject, *Their Paths Crossed Mine* (CNA, Johannesburg 1956) by Hans van Rensburg, leader of the Ossewabrandwag, and concludes with two pages exculpating and praising Mr B. J. Vorster, later prime minister.)

INDEX

INDEX